"I have a dream tha
children will one day l
where they will not be
color of their skin, but
of their character."

Martin Luther King

GW00703177

I have a dream
words to change the world

- MOTIVATE your pupils to write and appreciate poetry.
- INSPIRE them to share their hopes and dreams for the future.
- BOOST awareness of your school's creative ability.
- WORK alongside the National Curriculum or the high level National Qualification Skills.
- Supports the *Every Child Matters - Make a Positive Contribution* outcome.
- Over £7,000 of great prizes for schools and pupils.

"When I was out there I was never ever
alone, there was always a team of people
behind me, in mind if not in body."
— Ellen MacArthur

Future Voices
Edited by Mark Richardson

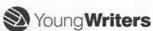

Young Writers

First published in Great Britain in 2006 by:
Young Writers
Remus House
Coltsfoot Drive
Peterborough
PE2 9JX
Telephone: 01733 890066
Website: www.youngwriters.co.uk

SB ISBN 1 84602 688 1

Foreword

Imagine a teenager's brain; a fertile yet fragile expanse teeming with ideas, aspirations, questions and emotions. Imagine a classroom full of racing minds, scratching pens writing an endless stream of ideas and thoughts . . .

. . . Imagine your words in print reaching a wider audience. Imagine that maybe, just maybe, your words can make a difference. Strike a chord. Touch a life. Change the world. Imagine no more . . .

'I Have a Dream' is a series of poetry collections written by 11 to 18-year-olds from schools and colleges across the UK and overseas. Pupils were invited to send us their poems using the theme 'I Have a Dream'. Selected entries range from dreams they've experienced to childhood fantasies of stardom and wealth, through inspirational poems of their dreams for a better future and of people who have influenced and inspired their lives.

The series is a snapshot of who and what inspires, influences and enthuses young adults of today. It shows an insight into their hopes, dreams and aspirations of the future and displays how their dreams are an escape from the pressures of today's modern life. Young Writers are proud to present this anthology, which is truly inspired and sure to be an inspiration to all who read it.

Contents

North Walsham High School, North Walsham

Becky Demmen (12)   49
David Wager (12)   50
Alistair Green (12)   50

Becky Demmen (12)	49
David Wager (12)	50
Alistair Green (12)	50
Liam Turton (12)	51
Anita Burrows (12)	51
Jessica Pratt (12)	52
Cristian Ilie (12)	52
Alex Tebble (12)	53
Charlotte Dawdry (12)	53
Siân Griffiths (13)	54
Rebecca Belshaw (15)	55
Hannah Siggee (12)	56
Becky Atyeo (12)	56
Gaby Tregidga (12)	57
Lynda Louise Wilson (12)	58
Lewis Barling (12)	58
Lisa-Marie Evers (12)	59
Billie Hurren (12)	59
Stacey Kent (12)	60
Lilly Brannan (12)	60
Tom Bayles (12)	61
Daniel Barber (12)	61
Anna Povey (12)	62
Kellie Ackerman (12)	62
Jake Isbell (13)	63
Thomas Belshaw (12)	63
Naomi Myhill (12)	64
Rhiannon Dack (11)	64
Luke Mulloy (13)	65
Thomas Baldock-Yaxley (12)	66
Chloe Bridges (12)	67
Jack Cresswell (12)	68
Francesca Lee (12)	69
Rebecca Pratt (12)	70
Beth Bridges (12)	71
Ben Chopping (12)	72

Perth Academy, Perth

Lisa McIntyre (14)	73
Eilidh Marnoch (13)	74
Holly Hunter (14)	75

Lisa Scrimgeour (13)   76
Hannagh Dellanzo (13)   77
Christopher Martin (14)   78
Claire Dryland (13)   79
Derek Chan (13)   80
Paul McPhee (14)   80
Joe Norris (13)   81
Lisa Bonthrone (13)   81
Kimberley White (13)   82
Zara Khan (14)   83
Klycia Carvalho (14)   84
Fergus Gill (14)   85
Andrew Christie (13)   86
Mark Jackson (14)   87
Louise Littlefair (14)   88
Kirsty MacDuff (14)   89

Redland School, Santiago
Maria Ignacia Troncaso Hugot (15)   90

Roundhay School Technology College, Leeds
Catriona Elliott (11)   91
Oliver Gularslan (12)   91
Emma Gilbank (12)   92
Emma Harris (12)   92
Kate Fraser (12)   93
Joshua Jones (12)   93
Haris Zubair (11)   94
Charan-Deep Rathore (12)   94
Sophie Fielding (12)   95
Emily Batty (12)   95
Hannah Nota (12)   96
Lewis Rudd (12)   96
Priya Chohan (12)   97
Nathanael Clarke (12)   97
Megan Chitty (12)   98
Joshua Dunwell (12)   98
Lauren Gibson (11)   99
Leah Edwards (11)   99
Emily Esgate (12)   100
Nashila Hussain (12)   100

Salia Hanif (12)   101
Emily Short (12)   101
Cindy Lee (11)   102
Tyron Jermaine Webster (12)   103
Sophie Ruse (11)   103
Shaquille Morton (12)   104
Ram Kalsy (12)   104
Elizabeth Johnson (12)   105
Justin Lau (12)   105

The Streetly School, Sutton Coldfield

Amber Robinson (11)	106
Kayleigh Middleton (12)	106
Hannah Deakin (13)	107
Jodie Edwards (12)	108
Hayley Peach (11)	108
Ryan Davis (12)	109
Beth Burgess (11)	109
Samantha Holyman (11)	110
Emily Freegard (11)	110
Zoe Darby (12)	111
Rachel Huckfield (12)	111
Jack Salter (12)	112
Grace Clusker (11)	112
Rebecca Snow (11)	113
James Duff (12)	113
Ben Perry (11)	114
Sophie Fisher (11)	115
Charlotte Craddock (12)	116
Scarlet Bowles (11)	116
Emily Rees (12)	117
Lucy Worrall (12)	117
Cree Lake (12)	118
Charlotte Turner (12)	119
Jack Fleming (11)	120
Daniel Whitehouse (12)	120
Shaun Wark (12)	121
Sarah Arrowsmith (11)	121
Matthew Nutt (11)	122
Ryan Bramwell (12)	122
Arjan Mangat (12)	123

Tonypandy Comprehensive School, Tonypandy

The Poems

I Have A Dream . . .

I want to be like Neil Armstrong
But not in space don't put me wrong.
I'd rather keep my feet on the ground
Where I can find a new place and be safe and sound.
I have a dream to go far,
Travel and see the world not just in a car.
Move around, walk and sightsee,
But not on my own, not just me.
Take my friends and family too,
And you can come along too.
Go to Paris, Sydney and Rome,
Go and see the Millennium Dome.
I love to have adventures because you don't know what's going to
happen next,
I love to look in books and look at all the pictures and text.
I would take my sketch pad and draw
At all the buildings that I saw.
I would love to take an all round the world tour,
I could visit Africa and see wild lions roar.

This is my dream to go and see the world!

Sophie Taylor (14)

Which Are You?

In American high schools there are popular kids,
They look good and are rich and people want to be like them.
But the real them is covered up,
All you see is a bullying mask,
But if you want to see the real them all you should do is ask.

In English secondary schools there are mean kids,
You wouldn't want to be like them
They aren't nice and the ones I know like rap
But inside their head there's a maze not a map.
They are confused and like to take it out on others,
The only antidote is a smile or two from the person they would
least think.

Then there are the good-goodies, the neeks, the freaks and the geeks,
They're international, universal.
In every city and every town,
All around the world,
Up and down,
On all the continents you'll find one,
And that, that is a real teenager.
I wish one day, maybe one day, everyone could be just like that.

Comfort Nwabia (14)

I Have A Dream

Cold, so cold,
alone in the darkness,
chains rattling, clanking,
biting into raw bloody flesh,
rats swarming around bare feet,
lonely,
so lonely . . .

Leaving family behind,
unprotected from the harshness of the world,
fearing life, living in terror,
dreaming of a better existence,
of a sunny, blissful place, far away,
brought back to Earth
to the harsh reality . . .

A warm glow on his face,
soothing pain, wiping away tears,
an extended angelic hand,
hand in hand, half-life, half-dream,
surrendering to paradise,
leaving the nightmare,
living the dream . . .

Natasha Lowther (13)
Haberdashers' Monmouth School for Girls, Monmouth

I Have A Dream

Walk in someone's shoes, see yourself.
You sit, blocking people's way, muttering,
people look at you in disgust, shaking their heads,
but you, you ignore them, concentrating on keeping out the cold.
Suddenly, someone takes pity, throws you a shining coin,
you grab at it, disturbing the pile of dogs resting beside you.
You get up, dragging blankets, a rucksack trailing on the ground,
and an assortment of things from long ago before it all changed.

You leave your doll, your bed, your home, walk away.
Cut your hair, pierce your nose, an eyebrow, and your lip.
You try to write a note, but can't, so you don't bother.
You leave in the dead of night, only your best friend knowing
where you've gone . . . but she doesn't . . . not really,
because all you said was that you'd had enough,
not that you were serious . . .

So you run . . . get the train into London, then you get the tube . . .
It's early morning now, the rush hour's only half an hour away . . .
But you don't care . . . all you care about is to get away from those
girls, the ones who teased you, pushed you around, stuck gum in
your hair . . . those ones.

But then you jump back into yourself . . . and then you spot it . . .
this morning's papers, your face splashed all over the tabloids . . .
and it's only then that you realise what you've done . . .
So you use your last £10, and get on the train, not knowing what
to expect when you get home . . .

And then when you arrive, you're enveloped in a hairspray
and cheap lipstick hug, your auntie, then your dad asks you where
you've been, but you don't reply, the thing that chokes you the most
is the new addition lying in her carrycot . . . a kitten, the one you
admired when you first saw her, but your mum said no . . .
and here she is in your living room,

You sit down on the sofa . . . and she leaps in your arms,
and you know . . .

You're home.

Alice Boxall (13)
Haberdashers' Monmouth School for Girls, Monmouth

I Have A Dream

I had a dream last night,
It wasn't very long,
But it was very comforting,
But it was also quite disturbing.

A close friend of mine was there,
And I was there as well,
We were in a drama class,
Getting along as usual.

All of a sudden it changed,
She turned against me,
Suddenly I'm falling,
Into the big pit of Hell.

An angel lifts me from my fall,
On the wings of love,
I'm rescued, I'm safe,
No longer in that hell.

The angel drops me down
Into a meadow with daisies and sunflowers,
There is a willow tree with ribbons and a swing,
Welcome to my special place; my lovely little haven.

I sit on the swing under the tree,
My legs swinging backwards and forwards,
My hair gleaming in the sun,
My dress rippling in the wind.

I never knew what happened next,
I will never dream that dream again,
But tomorrow will bring another dream,
Another life, another fantasy.

Mia Goddard (12)
Haberdashers' Monmouth School for Girls, Monmouth

The Dreams Of A Prisoner

The light is shining through the bars
Beyond, the misty, dew-soaked grass
Is calling out, enticing me
Towards the dream of being free

Once upon a time, I walked
Outside those bars, I laughed and talked
But all my thoughts wind back to hell
This cold and dusty prison cell

Twenty years ago, they stole
My life, and into this dark hole
They pushed me, shoved me, and that day
Hell arrived and came to stay

My dreams are of what could have been
I could have done, I could have seen
Then grim reality takes hold
And grasps me in her icy fold

And yet, my dreams are what I am
All the rest is just a sham
Waiting, waiting, silently
For the day when I am free.

Sophie Beckett (12)
Haberdashers' Monmouth School for Girls, Monmouth

I Have A Dream

I have a dream to get everybody to like each other,
No one would fight,
No one would care,
No one would yell or shout.

People would talk to strangers,
Take care of old people in the street,
Raise money for charities,
Even for your hometown or local school.

I have a dream that everybody would be the same,
Disabled, black or white,
People that are geeks, dull or don't want to learn,
Bullies, people who get bullied.

They are all the same, no different to
Me or *you!*

Theo Powell (15)
John Beddoes School, Presteigne

I Have A Dream

In my dream,
Everyone is part of the same team,
No one is an outsider,
Bullied or afraid.

In my dream
There are lakes and streams,
Flooding with peace,
Drowning everyone into a life of peacefulness.

In my dream,
No one screams,
For in my dream there's no such thing as fear!

This is where I wish to live!

Olivia Innes (14)
Maesydderwen Comprehensive School, Swansea

My Dream

My dream is to fly away,
Leave behind the troubles of the day.
My dream is to see what tomorrow brings,
It's an adventure to all new things.
My dream is to abolish crime,
And for the world to be just fine.
The world can be such hard going,
When there is so much fighting.
My poem isn't funny,
But it's not going to be all soppy.
So you ask me what my dream could be,
I don't know, it's only a dream.
But it could go like this . . .
Playing football for Arsenal and scoring all the goals.
Going to school and there being no rules.
Even breaking the world record for running,
Or get a black belt for kick-boxing,
I could go back in time to the war,
And stop it from prevailing anymore.
Well, whatever my dream may be,
I hope that you can see,
That black or white,
Green or pink,
We all look the same if you just think,
Just look inside your heart,
And you will see your dream come alive,
As that's what you desire,
But you won't be able to see your dream,
Until you just believe!

Natasja Marie Morgan (12)
Maesydderwen Comprehensive School, Swansea

I Have A Dream

I have a dream not to be in maths
Because it's really boring
Half the children are asleep
And my friend is snoring
All the shapes and numbers
Are starting to hurt my head
I sincerely wish
I was in my bed
The children doze
With heads on bags and desks
All except for the
Teacher's pets!
The wind outside the window
Starts to call my name
There are children out there playing
I wish I could do the same
I stare outside the window
At fresh air and grass
But I can't go there
Cos I'm stuck in class
All the paper aeroplanes
Fly above my head
Lots of different colours
Like orange, green and red
The teachers somehow stay awake
By reading magazines
While the children silently
Drift into their dreams
I have a dream
Not to be in maths!

Zoë Rees (12)
Maesydderwen Comprehensive School, Swansea

I Have A Dream

I have a dream that it will stop,
I have a wish to kill it off.
I want it all to go away,
I want people to have food each day.

I have a dream that no one will die,
I have a wish that no one does cry.
I want the rain to fall and fall,
I want the people to have it all.

I have a dream for children to grow,
I have a wish for them, one day to see snow.
I want them all to be healthy and well,
I want the children to have a story to tell.

I have a dream it will never come back,
I wish, one day, for poverty to stop!

Elin Evans (14)
Maesydderwen Comprehensive School, Swansea

I Have A Dream

I have a dream,
That I can wake up without the thought of prep scratching a dark
                                cave in the back of my mind,
That I can limp out of bed without an injury,
That I can push back the curtains and be certain of a memorable day.

I have a dream,
That I can climb the triangles of Egypt and watch Moses pleading,
That I can splash in the Thames and feel the flames of
                                September 1666,
That I can mount a horse's flanks and gallop to hear Troy fall.

I have a dream,
That I will never crush under pressure,
That I will never have unmarkable hate,
That as you read this you will enjoy it.

Tom Cox (13)
Marlborough College, Marlborough

I Have A Dream

I have a dream that I am in Cornwall,
I am on the golf course,
The sun beats down on me,
I put the ball on the tee,
They bet a fiver,
I pull out my driver,
I hit it well,
It all goes swell,
I look and lean,
It hits the green,
I walk along tall,
To meet my ball,
I pull out my putter,
My heart starts to flutter,
I hit the ball,
It starts to crawl,
It goes for the cup,
But then I wake up,
That was my dream.

Barnaby Hampel (13)
Marlborough College, Marlborough

I Have A Dream

I have a dream that one day poverty will not exist anymore,
I have a dream that everybody will have a family and be happy.
I have a dream that the world will be in complete peace.

I have a dream that Bush will not do any more stupid things,
I have a dream that France will win the World Cup,
I have a dream that Arsenal will win the Champions League.
I have a dream that Abramovich will go to jail and lose all his money.
I have a dream that Paris will become a beautiful city once again.

Charles Giesen (13)
Marlborough College, Marlborough

I Had A Dream

Snuggled up in my thick duvet,
I feel warm and content
Secure and content
Able to sleep safely

As I slip into sleep
I enter a world truly warm
The sun beating down on yellowing grass
A beautiful savannah, birds singing in the trees

But some are not as safe as me
I watch a herd of elephants crossing the plain
Huge and majestic, their tusks glinting
The tusks that will bring their death

For ivory poachers roam the land
Hiding in the shade of the great baobabs
Looking for victims to wreak havoc upon
For the sake of a few dollars

Within an hour the herd lies bleeding
Flies buzzing, vultures circling
I watch aghast as a mother's face is ripped apart
Her body spasming as her skin is ripped apart

I wake up, cold and clammy
Fearful of the surrounding darkness
Shocked by the injustice of it all
The mass death for a chess set.

James Lloyd (13)
Marlborough College, Marlborough

I Have A Dream

He wanted to be remembered,
For being the odd one out,
The one who stepped out of the box,
The one that made a difference.

He wanted to change the world,
Corny as it sounds.
He wanted to be renowned,
For being the one.

He wanted to save the people,
From everlasting pain,
His power would be famously unspoken,
His name would fill the world's minds.

He wanted to be not a saviour, but a silent hero.
His modesty would crush empires,
His love would slaughter fear,
His love would shake mountains.

He wanted to be admired in silence,
A man of his word,
To be revered by the greatest,
To be a standing stone in history.

He wanted to change the face of destiny,
Slicing a blade through its glorious looks.

Hamish Grant (13)
Marlborough College, Marlborough

I Have A Dream

I have a dream,
That the world won't go crazy,
But as foolish as it seems,
This world is much too lazy.

It's not that I'm a fighter,
But this place we call home,
Just might go up,
With a flick of a lighter.

I hope it'll be alright,
And cruelty, crime and violence,
Will no longer be a sight.

I still don't know,
Just what my dream shows,
But I won't delve further down,
Into a maze of impossibility.

Though I still think . . .

Oh how I hope,
That this world I visualise,
Might just shrink,
Into my real eyes.

Charlie Hockless (13)
Marlborough College, Marlborough

I Have A Dream

I often have a daydream to be granted just three wishes,
it is a futile dream I know, but maybe that is what dreams are for.
If I was granted just three wishes, I have thought it through,
I would wish I could fly with large white wings,
as fast as a fighter jet, yet have the agility of a hummingbird.
I wish I could breathe underwater (whilst still being able to breathe
on land as well, with the underwater speed and agility of a seal.
I wish that all the other wishes I have made would not be noticeable
to the naked eye when I wasn't taking advantage of them.

Courtney-Finn Burrow (13)
Marlborough College, Marlborough

I Have A Dream

I have a dream:
That the man will charge in
Flopping hair, bristling moustache
Peroxide blond. Diamond stud.
A blur of sweaty whites.

I have a dream:
That the ball will pitch on a length.
Outside off-stump. Blistering pace.
Inviting, tempting. Hit or leave?
Attack or defend? Hero or villain?

I have a dream:
That in a split second my foot comes out,
And across. Inside the line.
Toes pointing angelically out.
Bent knee, big stride, straight elbow, head over ball.
Bat pounces.

I have a dream:
That the blade comes down,
English willow, nature's finest.
Grains straight. Bat connects.

I have a dream:
That the leather and cork go far
Along the ground searing blades of grass and
Whistling ultrasonic sounds.
The twisted, knotted rope is disturbed.

That is my century.
The helmet flies off, feet leave the ground.
Emu and Kangaroo kiss patriotically,
As I mutter those sacred words:
Long live Australia!

Patrick Ford (14)
Marlborough College, Marlborough

I Have A Dream

Dreams of cleansing poor countries,
Of death, disease and poverty.
Dreams to be a bird, soaring,
Calm and effortlessly.

Dreams of unknown ancestors,
Of their life they tell me.
Dreams of nature's beauty,
Reefs, deserts and creatures in their plenty.

Dreams of possessing
Superhuman powers.
Dreams of preventing events,
Like the bombing of the Twin Towers.

Dreams to have the acting ability,
Of Sir Ian McKellen.
Dreams to be a musical genius,
Like men such as John Lennon.

Dreams to be as sporty,
As players such as Flintoff.
Dreams of meeting Nelson Mandela,
To him, my hat, I'd doff.

Dreams of reaching summits,
Like the one of Everest.
Dreams of being world-renowned,
As my nation's cleverest.

Dreams of having willpower,
Of men just like Lance Armstrong.
Dreams of being able to lie and dream,
All the ages long.

Matthew Capes (13)
Marlborough College, Marlborough

I Have A Dream

I have a dream,
That comes from a nightmare:
A village torn apart by war,
Abandoned buildings turned to rubble,
Showing signs of once being a home,
A shoe here, a pot there,
And then I hear the flies . . .

They buzz incessantly,
Feeding from death,
Dark flecks against a dark sky,
Animal carcasses litter the ground,
And the trail of death leads me to the field . . .

A field surrounded by razor wire,
That no longer supports a family,
But holds something more sinister than crops;
Just below the surface and out of sight,
One wrong step, a pressure pad,
The only harvest here will be death.

And then I wake.
But soon I am slipping away to a dream . . .

A small village, impoverished but happy,
Children playing, running through the streets,
A young girl taking her father's lunch to him,
Out on the field,
Where he works to bring in the crops,
Under a hot, bright sun.

One big difference through one small change.

Susannah Ponsford (13)
Marlborough College, Marlborough

I Have A Dream

The wind is screaming, trees whispering,
A lonely, destitute, free man enters,
A chair by the beaming fire is empty,
He does not take it,
He had seen the deep, rich colour of coal sitting on the men's skin.

Then a loving, intelligent, free woman enters,
She sees the seat, but to her despair
Does not sit down,
She had seen the gender of the table,
And how unjustly she was not comfortable sitting with men.

Finally a free stranger walks in,
They see the deserted chair and this time
The person sits down, with no shame or humiliation,
He had seen brothers;
Not their skin colour, or their gender, or their race,

This stranger is the man who knows God,
Who realises that
No longer should women be pushed to the side
For being a woman,
Never should scrutinising thoughts come into mind about race,

I have a dream for *equality,*
We are all free.

Alexandra Attard-Manché (13)
Marlborough College, Marlborough

I Have A Dream

One day,
A world content.
No jealousy or greed.

One day,
A world without suffering.
No pain or torture.

One day,
A hungerless world.
Where famines are mere memory.

One day,
A world free of crime.
Where all can live safely.

One day,
A fearless world.
Where no nightmares live.

For today
Is where children starve,
While mothers weep.

Today,
A world of horrors,
Where death stalks 'round the corner.

Philip Chope (13)
Marlborough College, Marlborough

I Have A Dream

I have a dream
To be a star
Celebrity actress
To go very far.
A famous boyfriend
The perfect hunk
Who gives to the poor,
Nuns and monks.

I wanna be in the movies
Stunningly pretty,
With a great personality,
Incredibly witty.

I want to live in Beverley Hills,
Have a house in Las Vegas,
Own a resort in Florida,
With no one to say to us,
'Do this! Do that!'
Stupid old prats!
'Don't make so much noise!
Move your Rolls Royce
From the front of our drive!
Your wealth makes us feel so deprived!'

But then
Look again
At current celebrities
Anorexic, bulimic,
Snorting dope with their homies.
Whinging and whining,
Cringing and crying,
Complaining, unretaining,
Faking and breaking,
What horrible people!
Bitching and fighting!
The 'perfect people'
Really aren't that enlightening!

'We are what you've made us!
You've slammed us,
You've shamed us!'
So maybe it'd be better
To stay simply anonymous.

Lettice Crawley Peck (14)
Marlborough College, Marlborough

I Have A Dream

I have a dream people see better than to mistreat animals,
To not keep dogs locked up,
And let them live like happy pups.
I dream people won't judge others by the colour of their skin,
Or rob people of their hard-earned money.

Can't people treat others equally?
Can't people find other ways to solve problems than to blow each
other up?
But what really makes me flip,
Is Liverpool's inability to win the Premiership,
Our strikers are the problem, can't you see?
But there's always a chance with Stevie G.
Everyone knows the world is full of wrong,
The 'Black-Eyed Peas' told us in a song,
I hope one day my dream will come true,
Meanwhile, I watch the corruption around me,
It's not something we can't see,
And it's not something we can't deal with,
Moving together is the key,
Gaining inspiration from Mandela and Ghandi,
We must sort out this mess,
And the world will be in harmony.

Charlotte James (13)
Marlborough College, Marlborough

Whatif?

(Based on 'Whatif' by Shel Silverstein)

Whatif you had no home,
No one to talk to on the phone?

Whatif you had no food to eat?
All you had was the ground for a seat.

Whatif you had no clean water,
And had to feed your six young daughters?

Whatif you had nothing at all?
All you had was a scruffy old doll.

Whatif you were me?
My name is Max and I am 30.

This is my life as *you* may not see,
So next time please give money to charity.

Heather Graham (14)
Mearns Castle High School, Newton Mearns

The World We Live In

Imagine a world where the homeless roam the streets for shelter,
Where people suffer because of their religion or race,
Where children work like slaves to earn nothing.

Imagine a world where refugees are treated like cold-blooded
                                                    criminals,
Where the majority are carelessly destroying the environment,
Where people are taught to raise their fists to get what they want.

Imagine a world where there are emaciated children
With hallowed faces and skeletal bodies, who pray that one day
Something good will happen, for once in their lives.

We don't need to imagine.
If you open your eyes,
You will see this is the world we live in.

Sub Mei Chan (14)
Mearns Castle High School, Newton Mearns

Your World, My World - Our World

Walking through the streets of Nairobi
I pass a lifeless body
Swarms of flies eating at rotting flesh.
A starving boy by its side
Tears at the corners of his eyes.

I remember just yesterday
I saw them singing
Along with the rest of the carnival
I remember just yesterday
I saw them smiling
Smiling and waving with the rest of the carnival
I remember just yesterday
How full of life they were, I remember

Walking through the streets of London
I pass a lifeless body
Swarms of flies amidst the McDonald's coffee.
A starving dog by its side
Eyes blinded by infection.

I remember just yesterday
I saw them performing
A large crowd had gathered
I remember just yesterday
I saw them smiling
Smiling and bowing as they were cheered
I remember just yesterday
How full of life they were, I remember

But what I can't remember
Is a day where none went starving!
That, I can't remember.

Sam Green (14)
Mearns Castle High School, Newton Mearns

Is This Right?

No food for energy after a long day in the sun,
Empty bellies and tired souls.
People starving to death, hunger taking over.
Children so thin that their bones can be seen through their flesh.
Is this right?
No water to quench an undying thirst,
No water supplies near home.
Having to walk miles in the exhausting heat only to find the water
                                                    is dirty.

No pump to purify diseased water.
Is this right?
No shelter, no home, nowhere to hide from the African heat
                                in the middle of a drought.
Sleeping on the streets with no clothes to keep you warm at night.
Nowhere to call home.
Is this right?
No schools, no books, nowhere to learn.
No qualifications to get a job.
No job to keep your family alive.
Having to beg in the raging heat just to bring in a little money.
Is this right?
Disease spreading, with no way to stop it.
Losing your family, loved ones and friends.
Is this right?

Heather Gardner (14)
Mearns Castle High School, Newton Mearns

The Winner

Coming home late at night
From every window blinks a light
Warm and welcoming, a friendly sight

Step inside, feel the heat
Music blaring, kind of neat
Radiator hot, warms the seat

Boiler pounding
TV sounding
No! TV's sounding

Computers on, email coming
Hairdryer wails, can hear it humming
Mobile set, that's it ringing

Overhead the plane is droning
Pylons high, sit there moaning
Masts are there, so we can go on phoning

Far away, trees are falling
For heavy logs they are a-hauling
No wonder planet Earth is taking a mauling!

On the meters, the dials are spinning
Gas and electric, sit there grinning
That's how we know, global warming's winning!

Kirsteen McPake (14)
Mearns Castle High School, Newton Mearns

Poverty

The heat is unbearable,
Stuck in this draught,
My sibling are crying,
I try so hard to help out.
I work so hard night and day,
Hoping to keep starvation at bay.

My baby sister's getting so thin,
I'd do anything to stop her from wailing,
It's too late now!
The most I can do is keep on praying.
Insects continue flying,
Surrounding the helpless and dying.

In my country money is unheard of
Water is as precious as gold,
The sun blazes down, scalding our skin,
There is no such thing as cold.
We hope and pray to God that these dreadful days will end,
And soon we will have money to save our lives and to spend.

Rachael Doherty (14)
Mearns Castle High School, Newton Mearns

Untitled

There is so much destruction in this world,
Because of two small
Insignificant things.

People are discriminated against,
Made to feel inferior,
And only know how to feel hate,
Pain and anger.

Black and white.
Two simple words,
Overrated though, unimportant.

Fiona Stevenson (14)
Mearns Castle High School, Newton Mearns

When Will The World Learn?

When will the world learn?
Men, women and children
sprawled in the disease-infested streets of Africa,
while the government fat-cats lap it up,
living in style.

When will the world learn?
Money is raised and aid arrives,
but Mugabe and co squander it all on self-improvement.
Millions of pounds just *disappear*
- Where?

When will the world learn?
Malnourishment spreads like a disease,
whilst governors and senates eat like the *kings* they believe they are;
Driving out those who pale in complexion.
Justice? Democracy?
The world thinks not.

When will the world learn?

Ross Atkin (14)
Mearns Castle High School, Newton Mearns

Untitled

Why is racism still an issue?
Black or white, we should all be equal.
Why should colour determine who we are?
Black or white, we are all still people.

Do you understand why people are racist?
Black or white, we should all be equal.
Is it not what's underneath that counts?
Black or white, we are all still people.

People are racist, we just don't all admit it.
Black or white, do you think we are all equal?
People do judge books by their covers.
Black or white, do you think we are all still people?

Abby Shields (14)
Mearns Castle High School, Newton Mearns

Equality Of Life

Is society flawed?
Drugs and crime run rampant,
Death and blood run free,
As the water in a river.
Is society flawed?
People try to kid themselves,
Racism is gone,
But until we all do something about it,
It shall remain a scar on the face of humanity.
Is society flawed?
Unless we fix it,
The people burning in the inferno of injustice,
Shall rise up against the corrupt.
If you think society isn't flawed,
Prove me wrong and try to stop injustice,
Do not be racist for all people are equal,
Is society flawed?
If it weren't, people would donate money,
To charities to build a better world.
If society wasn't flawed,
People wouldn't casually cast aside their litter,
And pollute the planet.
Is society flawed?
Even in peace,
Governments make weapons to maim their equals,
Instead we should put effort into severing injustice.
Try and fix society,
So we can turn Earth into the utopia our ancestors imagined,
There, everyone from the poorest beggar to the richest entrepreneur,
Would bask in the equality of life.

Michael Reid (14)
Mearns Castle High School, Newton Mearns

Make A Change

The world keeps revolving,
And the pain keeps coming,
People hurting, killing, dying,
And still the pain keeps coming.

The world is growing warmer,
But this crisis is ignored,
By ignorant politicians,
Who just won't learn.

America heroically herding troops into Iraq,
Lying to cover their own greed,
It's the oil they really want,
Zimbabwe is the country in need.

The world keeps revolving
And the pain will keep on coming,
People hurt, kill and die,
And their pain will keep on coming.

Child abuse, terrorism, genocide,
From devastating situations we try to hide,
Refuse to accept that some matters are beyond our control.

Racism, inequality, bigotry,
What will it take to make the world finally see,
That this 'perfect' planet will no longer be,
Until we can make a change?

And so the world keeps revolving,
And the pain keeps coming,
People hurting, killing, dying
And still their pain keeps coming . . .

Emma Davidson (15)
Mearns Castle High School, Newton Mearns

Does It Ever Wake You In The Night?

Does it ever wake you in the night,
The fact that our world is in great plight?
We hurt, maim, kill and destroy all in our path
Cruelty covers the world like an evil shroud of pain
Do you let it pass you by?

Does it ever wake you in the night,
The fact that thousands die each day,
At the hands of those in whose leadership they have no say?
Will you allow this to slip past?

Does it ever wake you in the night,
The fact that death is the easy option,
For millions of little children
Whose blood and tears give you your perfect labels?
Can you honestly not care?

Does it ever wake you in the night,
The fact that beautiful species from the dawn of time
Are lost before discovered?
Will you stand for this?

Look out your window at the sight,
And then we'll see if it wakes you in the night.

Siobhan Murphy (15)
Mearns Castle High School, Newton Mearns

Sectarianism

Two colours, blue and green,
That's what you may think,
But some think they mean,
Something that has no link.

Rangers or Celtic?
Is what they want to know,
If you give the wrong answer,
You'd better run fast . . . not slow.

Ibrox or Parkhead?
Where do you go?
Is that supporter,
Your friend or foe?

Blue or green?
You decide.
There is no place
To run and hide.

Love the game,
Not the team.
And no one should care,
If you're blue or green.

Laura Mulligan (14)
Mearns Castle High School, Newton Mearns

Racism

The world is ever changing,
Yet we all stay the same.
Just because of one man's differences,
We give him hate and pain.

The world is ever changing,
Yet we all stay the same.
We treat each other differently,
Due to crazy claims.

The world is ever changing,
Yet we all stay the same.
Many people die tonight,
Because of racial blame.

The world is ever changing,
Yet we all stay the same.
There is a worldly evil,
Racism is its name.

The world is ever changing,
It's time we changed our game!

Leon O'Rourke (14)
Mearns Castle High School, Newton Mearns

Difference Of Two Worlds

We think of silence as no noise,
No whispers, no thoughts, not even a pin dropped on the floor,

Yet just because people believe different things,
Have different coloured skin,
Live in another part of the world,

Their silence is of noise,
The silence of shouts and screams,
Full of gunshots, explosions, tanks, grenades,

But if it were to stop,
To them it would be unnatural.
If it were to start,
For us it would be destruction.

Our silence is their heaven,
Our hell, their silence,

The same world,
And not so different,
So why are their lives a misery and full of devastation?

Jenna Cowan (14)
Mearns Castle High School, Newton Mearns

Racism

War, what is war?
War is what makes people sad,
It makes people lose their dad,
It gives the government land,
And every speck of sand.

War is power,
When really it should be for freedom and love,
It is expensive and violent,
And turns the whole nation silent.

Poverty covers the world
People suffer, people die
But people should stop and think
What the hell are we doing?
Poverty is a result of war
War is a result of greed
How could anyone commit such a deed?

Terrorism scares people to the bone
And turns their thoughts and fears to stone
Terrorism is throughout the nation
And leaves countries with bad temptations
Can they be brought under control?
Can they be captured?
However, one question is still to be answered
When will they next attack?
But unfortunately, that is an unknown fact.

Racism covers the world in a rash
It pollutes the air like cloudy ash.
Why are people racist?
Why do they make people suffer?
Is it to make themselves look big or bold
Or to make them look superior?
Only one thing can be said, and that is we are all equal
And feature in the same sequel.

Ryan Higgins (15)
Mearns Castle High School, Newton Mearns

Hope

It's been centuries
Human kind has suffered
From depravity, foolishness, brutality, selfishness
Innocent people have died
From war and poverty, sickness and slavery
Helpless countries have struggled
From exploitation, pollution, addiction, starvation

There's not one more or less unworthy
That you could leave as a legacy
For the next generation's destiny

The most unbearable is a child mistreated
Abused heartlessly, tortured barbarically
And their insane persecutors released
From their crime and cruelty
With total impunity

So why still wake up and believe
In a better tomorrow
When we just want to sleep
Ending life in deep sorrow?

But it's been centuries
Leaders have inspired
Justice and honesty, peace and charity
Rosa Parks, Mother Teresa
Luther King, Nelson Mandela
Determined, awoke all blind nations
Persisted to fight discriminations

Tell us wonderful stories
About courage, faith and glories
That bring sunshine to each morning
And hope for love everlasting.

Roxane Picard (14)
Mearns Castle High School, Newton Mearns

Life Of Terror

Terrorist bombings, murder
Innocents slaughtered
Survivors living a life of terror

Vandalism, kidnappings, muggings
Destroying lives
Hard work shattered

The modern world
Is a world where people
No longer want to live

Merciless deaths
Crime rules the streets
Everyone's life is
A life lived in fear
A life with little hope
A life of terror.

Joe West (13)
North Walsham High School, North Walsham

Oppressed Animals

They live in the deserts, they live in the trees,
From snakes and spiders, to tiny little bees.
They swim in the oceans, they glide over clouds,
How different this is to the big city crowds.
How it should be, is as *free as free,*
Animals deserve life, just like you and me.
They're locked up in cages and beaten with sticks,
They want to escape but are kept there by twits!
Shouldn't they be free to do just as they please?
Why do we do this? Please set them free.

Samuel David Woolcock (13)
North Walsham High School, North Walsham

I Have A Dream

I have a dream.
That animals are treated fair,
Humans don't seem to worry,
Not even when animals yelp, they don't care.

It happens all over the world,
No one country is better than others.
Animals are just hurled,
They don't even get covers.

I have a dream,
That there is no animal cruelty.
Why doesn't everyone work as a team?
No one complains and calls people like that faulty.

I have a dream,
Dogs are in cages too small.
All the animals always scream,
Even kittens are crammed up against the wall.

I have a dream,
If I were rich I would set them all free.
I bet if I rescued them, their faces would beam,
The animals and I together would be as happy as could be.

Charlotte Marriott (11)
North Walsham High School, North Walsham

Think

T he voice in the crowd
H aving a dream
I n your world
N ever give up
K now the truth.

Chris Beatty (13)
North Walsham High School, North Walsham

I Have A Dream . . .

I have a dream,
I dream the trees will stay,
That there will still be a running stream,
And that the animals will not stray,

I have a wish,
I have a dream,
Please stop hunting and killing the fish,
And let's continue the sun's welcoming beam,

The sun has been provoked,
Death faces the trees,
Growing is the smoke,
Sadly, the buildings will not be ceased,

The cows in herds,
Will eat no more green,
And no more high homes for the birds,
I have a dream,

The owls will no longer hoot,
But this can all be halted,
The humans will gain more loot,
And the chickens will continue to be salted,

I have a dream,
I dream the trees will stay,
That there will still be a running stream,
And that the animals will not stray.

John Seaman (12)
North Walsham High School, North Walsham

Questions

Destroying confidence
How would I feel?
Gone in seconds
How would I feel?
Despairing, depressed
How would I feel?

As low as dirt
That's how you felt
Lost in hurt
That's how you felt
Handful of pills
Because of how you felt

Now you're dead
How do they feel?
No thoughts in your head
How do they feel?
No more words said
How do they feel?

Malicious words jeered
Do they regret?
The way people leered
Do they regret?
Are they upset?
I hope they regret.

Anna Bodymore (13)
North Walsham High School, North Walsham

I Think

When I walk through the corridor, I think,
Staring at the ceiling, staring at the floor, I think,
What if the world were different
It's all rhymes, rhythms, it's all consistent
It's all about how we live our lives,
Time is ticking, it's quarter to five.
When I walk through the corridor, I think
Staring at the ceiling, staring at the floor, I think

The world is sinking under
It's asking for help, it's the thunder
The destructions are the tears
People are scared, they're full of fear
When I walk through the corridor, I think,
Staring at the ceiling, staring at the floor, I think,
It's too late to change what has already been done
In a way we've lost, in a way we've won

Can you think of a way to help?

Georgina Harrod (13)
North Walsham High School, North Walsham

Victims Of Poverty

Poverty seizes its victims
It holds its grip for life
Its victims struggle to escape
But they are bound with ties.

Poverty causes immense destruction
It's a serial killer, by way of filth
And infections, dirty and deadly disease
One that needs to be stopped.

Victims stuck, helpless, can't get free
They can't get away from the torture
Just patiently waiting for a lifeline
But nothing comes, just waiting, still waiting . . .

Ben Dixon (13)
North Walsham High School, North Walsham

Government

The government is like a bowling ball,
Not taking action unless pushed.
The government is like a matchstick,
It snaps at the slightest touch.
The government is like a bully,
Stealing our lunch money.
The government is like a student,
Easy to teach and tell what to do.
The government is like a fish on land,
Flapping about hopelessly on the ground.
The government is dreadful.
The government is disgraceful.
The government is damnable,
The government is disgusting.
But could it be amazing?

Tim Burden (13)
North Walsham High School, North Walsham

Make It Stop

Can't you see this terrible torture,
That's known as wrong but never ends?
Constant punishment of animals and people,

I have a dream to make it stop.

You're too wrapped up in your own life to notice,
One hit, two hits, three hits won't hurt.
Everyone buries their heads in the sand,

I have a dream to make it stop.

There is such a thing as fate,
Karma will come and see you one day
Will there be someone to stick up for you?

I have a dream to make it stop.

Charlotte Smith (13)
North Walsham High School, North Walsham

I Have A Dream . . .

I have a dream . . .
that animals will have rights.

Animals are not free,
they are tagged and kept in cages.

Farm animals lie cramped,
watching, crying as their young are taken away.

The lion in the zoo paces up and down,
bored, depressed.
It longs to live in the wild.

The animal in the abattoir senses it's going to die,
painfully, horrifically.

These animals deserve better.
They don't deserve this torture.
They don't deserve pain and suffering.

Animals want rights.
Animals want better lives.

Isabella List (13)
North Walsham High School, North Walsham

I Have A Dream

Different countries have different quantities of money,
Different countries have different types of currency,
Different countries have different amounts of ability,
Education, a lot of orphans don't get any.
Why is the world so unjust?
Why is the world so unfair?
Why has everyone given up all trust?
Everyone having to grin and bear!

Peggy Baldwin (13)
North Walsham High School, North Walsham

I Have A Dream

I have a dream which is unspoken.
A dream which is real.
This dream should not be broken
And this is how I feel.

I have a dream that dogs shouldn't die.
People should be kind.
No wonder most are shy.
There's niceness out there somewhere, one day we will find.

I have a dream no cats should be shot.
Their lives shouldn't be as dull as lead.
I think not.
No cats should be lying dead.

I have a dream which is unspoken.
A dream which is real.
This dream should not be broken
And this is how I feel.

Charlotte Williams (12)
North Walsham High School, North Walsham

Stop!

Stop hunting the animals of the world.
Stop killing them off for money.
They're becoming extinct, one by one they're dying!
The animals of the world are crying.
Stop hunting the animals of the world.
Stop using animal meat and giving it to your dog for a treat.

Stop hunting the animals of the world.

Shaun Wardle (12)
North Walsham High School, North Walsham

I Had A Dream

I had a dream
In which all animals were safe
And treated like human beings
And weren't put to race.

I had a dream
That animals like cats
Weren't tested with cream
Or had to wear hats.

I had a dream
Where pets including frogs
Weren't captured by teams
Or trodden on by dogs.

I had a dream
In which all animals were safe
And treated like human beings
And weren't put to race.

Charlotte Fitzgerald (12)
North Walsham High School, North Walsham

Racism

People should all be treated the same
But some people feel that they are in shame
They shouldn't be different because of their colour.

Some people just don't care
But others find it very unfair
Why are people racist to others?

When people abuse in such a way
Sometimes others feel dismay
People don't just abuse verbally.

If every person was treated fair
And everyone found that they could share
They'd all get along alright.

Chris Wooden (13)
North Walsham High School, North Walsham

I Have A Dream

I have a dream,
That animals have rights,
Some dogs are drowned in streams,
Some cats are made to have frights.

I have a dream,
That animals have rights,
Some birds have to balance on a beam,
Some hamsters are never fed at night.

I have a dream,
That animals have rights,
Some rats are killed right at the seam,
Some voles are strangled with tights.

I have a dream,
That animals are treated right,
No more drowning in streams
And no more animal frights.

Amy Bicknell (11)
North Walsham High School, North Walsham

Cancer

Cancer's a disease that eats you alive.
It rips you to pieces, no chance to survive.
You come to the end in an excruciating way.
It kills hearts from the core in every broken day.
Money is needed to work out the cure.
To help all those people with hearts, oh so pure.
If you know someone who died, you know how it feels
To watch someone finish, feeling pain so unreal.
Help cure cancer by donating some cash.
Stop the pain of cancer, hit, whip and thrash.

Saskia Coleman (13)
North Walsham High School, North Walsham

I Have A Dream

I have a dream
To help animals be free,
Not left in a freezing cold stream,
Not left starving without tea.

I have a dream,
Animals need to be cared for,
Not left underneath a beam,
Before another kitten gets thrown against a door.

I have a dream,
Bears should be free to eat their honey,
Before animals turn into whipped cream
All of this for a bit of money.

I have a dream,
And it's turning blue,
And if you help me raise money for this theme,
And then maybe, just maybe, it might come true!

Jade Hewitt (11)
North Walsham High School, North Walsham

Racism

Black, coloured, whatever you say,
Let's stop racism straightaway,
Evil people so, so harsh,
If you're black, they'll just laugh.

Not all of them are vile,
All of them would soon smile,
Kick out racism,

Yes, today, get it out

   This very day!

Sean West (13)
North Walsham High School, North Walsham

I Have A Dream

I have a dream
That nobody would kill
That would be like cream
And then they wouldn't have to have a will.

I have a dream
That nobody would stab
That would make my face beam
Then nobody would have to pick up the tab

I have a dream
That there would be no abuse
Then we would all be a team
And investigators wouldn't have to deduce.

I have a dream
That nobody would bully
Then nobody would be mean
And people could enjoy life fully.

Ryan Bullock (12)
North Walsham High School, North Walsham

I Have A Dream

I have a dream
That you can play sport, whether short or tall
That children everywhere will belong to a team
I have a dream that every child will play sport from Montreal
to Senegal.

Football, basketball, dodgeball or any sport you choose
I have a dream that every town and village has somewhere
to play sport

It doesn't matter if you win or lose
I have a dream to play sport on the street or on a court.

Ryan Beeson (12)
North Walsham High School, North Walsham

Time Is Running Out

Time is running out,
The ozone layer dying.
Time is running out,
The world like an oven.
Time is running out,
Destroying the environment.
Time is running out.

Effects will be devastating,
If you don't do anything.
Seawater rising,
Countries are fading.

Time is running out,
Chaos is building.
Time is running out,
Cars keep on driving.
Time is running out,
The carnage is disgraceful.
Time is running out.

The world will be a shadow
Of its former self,
If you just sit there,
Too idle to care.

Time is running out.

Laura Hunter (13)
North Walsham High School, North Walsham

If I Had A Dream

If I had a dream, the dream would be . . .
to encourage everyone to achieve their dream,
wouldn't it be nice to see every human being,
living side by side in harmony?
This would truly be a wonderful dream.

Alice Gardner (12)
North Walsham High School, North Walsham

My Family

I have a dream,
About my special family,
Flowing down a stream,
But very happily.

I have a dream,
About a bother,
But it seems,
It's with my lover.

I have a dream,
About a place,
Where we can be a team,
To have some family space.

I have a dream,
About family fun,
Strawberries and cream,
And a holiday in the sun.

Kelly Brown (12)
North Walsham High School, North Walsham

Poverty Kills

P hasing out this pit of despair.
O ften harder than it sounds.
V ery volatile, yet nothing is done.
E very second I feel a renewed loss.
R elentless plague across my land.
T orture. Why don't you lend a hand?
Y ou have more power than you know.

K illing my friends and my family.
I llnesses left uncured.
L earn to help me.
L earn to save me.
S omething small to you is lifesaving to us!

Becky Demmen (12)
North Walsham High School, North Walsham

I Have A Dream

I have a dream
that I will have the skills,
to play for a professional football team
who will pay the bills.

I have a dream
of being class,
when I play for my team
I will hit a fantastic pass.

We'll have some games that are tight
for me and my team,
the opposition will fight
but I have a dream.

I have a dream
there are a few blurs,
I'm playing for a team
it must be Spurs.

David Wager (12)
North Walsham High School, North Walsham

War Is Stupid

I have a dream,
To change the world,
To stop all the fighting on the Earth.
Oh, war is stupid!

All the killing,
All the eradication,
All the destruction.
Oh, war is stupid!

War is brutal,
Inhumane and horrendous.
War is stupid!

Alistair Green (12)
North Walsham High School, North Walsham

Death Is The End

I have a dream,
To stop the poverty.
Let the poor people sing,
Not scream and shout.

From pain and suffering and demise,
They must struggle.
They depend on us,
To stop the starvation
And for them to be happy.

I have a dream,
To stop the death, the pain, the suffering
And to make them happy.
Death is the end.
Life is the new beginning!

Liam Turton (12)
North Walsham High School, North Walsham

Homeless

Picture this:
Being all alone on a cold dark street.
Picture this:
Screaming for food or, at least, some clean water to drink.
Picture this:
Shivering with fear, for you are scared of the people who have
                                                    hurt you.

Picture this:
Being scarred with sadness.
Picture this:
Only having a thin, tattered blanket to huddle into.
Picture this:
Being all alone on a cold dark street.

Anita Burrows (12)
North Walsham High School, North Walsham

I Have A Dream

I have a dream.
Endangered are polar bears,
They are pure cream.
Pandas all shedding their tears
Flowing down in a stream.
Why don't we care?

I have a dream
We can be fair.
Let's stop now and calm the pandas' tears.
Homeless are polar bears,
Soon they will run out of steam.
I wish we would be fair,
And it wasn't a dream.

I have a dream.
Pandas are safe and like fresh cream.
Calm and safe are polar bears.

I have a dream.
No more people without cares.
Thoughtfulness fills my dream.

Jessica Pratt (12)
North Walsham High School, North Walsham

I Have A Dream

I have a dream to save the world,
To save the bees.
I have a dream to save you all,
By saving the trees.
If you're rich or poor,
Want less or more,
Spend loads of time in a pool,
Or play golf like Guilotmore.
Love nature more!

Cristian Ilie (12)
North Walsham High School, North Walsham

Hold On

This world may be cruel but you don't have to leave,
You're locking up these things inside, you and your hopes are thin,
Your dreams are disappearing like water down the drain,
And no one seems to care.

You're feeling grave, you're feeling isolated,
And you think you're on a dead end road.
Your mother's gone and your father's left you,
This pain you cannot bear.

These days. These days you feel alone,
And at nights you can't sleep at all. Hold on!
'Cause we all bleed the same way as you,
And we all have the same things to go through.

So, don't stop looking, you're one step closer,
Don't stop searching, it's not over,
Hold on,
If you feel like letting go,
Hold on!

Alex Tebble (12)
North Walsham High School, North Walsham

I Have A Dream!

My claws, scratching
My teeth, snatching
As I try to struggle
Free!
The cane, bashing
The whip, lashing
Oh why does it have to be
Me?
My skin, worn,
My heart, torn
It's animal cruelty, can't you
See?

Charlotte Dawdry (12)
North Walsham High School, North Walsham

Undone

She's been in her room for hours,
Just lying on her bed,
With worries the size of towers,
Building in her head.

This world which she lives in,
This so-called comfort zone,
Why is it being so confusing,
Leaving her own identity unknown?

'Why can't I look like them?'
She asks herself in vain,
'Why is she so ready to condemn?
I just want to be the same!'

Is she the only one who feels this way
Or do we all as well?
I mean how do you feel today?
Do you want to tell?

But it shouldn't be like this,
Come on, you know I'm right,
We should give insecurity a miss.
It's time to stop the fight.

So now the time has come,
It's time to take a stand,
Let's unite as one
And join hand in hand.

Even to the girl, crying in her room,
Yes, and also to you too.
My message here is clear . . .

The most important person is you!

Siân Griffiths (13)
North Walsham High School, North Walsham

Believe

Believe your heart,
And follow your soul.
Discard your head,
And enjoy this bore.
We don't live long,
We always move on,
So make that merry, merry song.
Join the dance,
Make up the steps,
And play the game,
The game to life.
Make your rules,
And the path you choose,
You just can't lose.
Don't expect the steps not to fall away,
And your feet not to pay,
Just don't be afraid.
Leave the large door open,
And don't close the windows either.
Retrieve the music,
Discard the silence,
Feel the warmth,
Yet know the shadows.
Walk away and you
Will never see the light of day.
Argue for what you see,
Have faith in yourself,
Be who you are,
Not the person they want to see.
You just have to believe.

Rebecca Belshaw (15)
North Walsham High School, North Walsham

I Have A Dream

I have a dream
Of a polar bear,
His teeth that gleam
As he stares.
I have a dream
Of him and his lair,
If we work as a team
We can make people care.
I have a dream
That he soon won't be there,
Because people are mean
And if we don't help,
He will become rare.
I have a dream
Of a polar bear,
His teeth that gleam
As he stares.

Hannah Siggee (12)
North Walsham High School, North Walsham

I Have A Dream

I have a dream to change the world,
To get rid of hatred and anger,
Broken hearts, grieving and sad,
I have a dream to change the world.

Prejudice, racial hate, sexism,
All black-hearted, hateful and cruel,
No needed in this world of passion,
I have a dream to change the world.

I wish I could change the world,
Where people are pure and truthful,
Life full of joy, happiness and jubilation,
I have a dream to change the world . . .

Becky Atyeo (12)
North Walsham High School, North Walsham

If I Had A Dream

If I had a dream,
I'd dream people could realise,
That everyone isn't what they seem,
So they wouldn't be so surprised.

If I had a dream,
Everywhere there would be love,
And instead of there being a beam,
Lies would just fly away like a dove.

I had it all,
Two families I loved a lot,
Just for one person to have a ball,
Made me wish I could forget.

The one person most close to me,
Was abused,
I wish life were just free,
And that she and I weren't so confused.

Most of all, I felt betrayed,
By my own dad!
Whilst I was lying there, afraid,
I felt really bad.

As I was crying and shaking,
Realising what I had heard,
My other stepsister was awaking,
Just by hearing that one important word.

I'd wish we could still be a team,
And go back to how things used to be,
If I had a dream,
All these things wouldn't have happened to me.

Then I realised I'd been a fool,
If I had a dream,
Not everything would be run by rules,
And life wouldn't be so mean.

Gaby Tregidga (12)
North Walsham High School, North Walsham

I Have A Dream Of Happiness

I have a dream,
There's no pain, poverty or prejudice.

Life is full of laughter,
Not affliction or suicides.
Every day people face:
'Dad's fist is a cannon powering into my face!'
'No food tonight.'
'Her hand lashing me, like a leather whip.'
'I hate you: you blacks are all the same.'

Why?

Why can't it be more like . . .
Happiness amongst families and friends,
Equal amounts of food and money,
Races calm and supporting each other?

I have a dream,
There's no pain, poverty or prejudice,
Fight back!

Lynda Louise Wilson (12)
North Walsham High School, North Walsham

Poverty

Poverty is just the beginning
With no food to stay healthy
Hardly any water to keep living
Money is spent on roads and cars
When there are people who just want to live.
The pain and hunger of starving children
I have a dream that everyone will live fairly
Everyone has a chance to live
But soon comes death
Everywhere people dying
Poverty is just the beginning
Death is the end!

Lewis Barling (12)
North Walsham High School, North Walsham

Bullying

Jeopardised by fear
Threatened to the skin
Unbreakable hold that lies
Deep within.

How do we help the victim
To get their confidence back?
How do we help the bully
To get the likeable side they lack?

We can beat bullies by
Showing the stress they create,
We can help the victim by
Telling them they're not bully bait.

Jeopardised by fear
Threatened to the skin
Unbreakable hold that no longer
Lies deep within.

Lisa-Marie Evers (12)
North Walsham High School, North Walsham

I Have A Dream!

I have a dream,
That the world had peace,
That conflict between countries would stop.
War is wicked and wrong, an almighty tornado ruining people's lives.
The crimes committed like murder and racism,
Should be stopped and punished, when they're done.
People want calm streets at night, not angry fights from drunken
                              people, they make our towns look cruel.
They smash up cars and break windows,
That's not the way we want our world.
We want peace like a silent, open room.
We can't tolerate this, it's wrong.
We want peace.

Billie Hurren (12)
North Walsham High School, North Walsham

I Have A Dream

I have a dream, that the world is fair,
And no one's bullied or teased,
I have a dream, that people do care,
And people are nice, not mean.

I have a dream, that the bullies stop,
And realise they are bad and wrong,
I have a dream, that they say they're sorry
And the victims become more strong.

I have a dream, that people aren't afraid,
Because they know they can trust others,
I have a dream, that even at night,
They can go out without fright.

I have a dream, and it can come true,
And it will do, with the help from you.

Stop bullying!

Stacey Kent (12)
North Walsham High School, North Walsham

Life In Poverty

If it's too hot, we have air conditioning.
If it's too cold, we have central heating.
If we are hungry, we raid the cupboards.
If we are ill, we call a doctor.
So why is it . . .
If it's too hot, they put up with it?
If it's too cold, they live with it?
If they are hungry, they starve?
If they are ill, they die?
But this can be helped,
Education, health and clean water
Can change a life in Africa,
No more strife,
Change a life,
Help build a future!

Lilly Brannan (12)
North Walsham High School, North Walsham

Killers

People use these again and again,
Weapons and drugs are killers.
People are eliminated again and again,
Weapons and drugs are killers.
Families cry again and again,
Weapons and drugs are killers.
Lives are shattered again and again,
Weapons and drugs are killers.
People lose their minds again and again,
Weapons and drugs are killers.
People beg again and again,
Weapons and drugs are killers.
People suffer again and again,
Weapons and drugs are killers.

Why?

Tom Bayles (12)
North Walsham High School, North Walsham

I Had A Dream

I had a dream
That there was a freedom for passion
And a liberty for anarchy.

I had a dream
That living life to the full was a truth
And you had a right to your beliefs.

I had a dream
That speaking out for your rights,
Wasn't a death penalty.

I had a dream.

Daniel Barber (12)
North Walsham High School, North Walsham

Stop The Hunger

I have a dream to change the world,
To stop the hunger of poor people.

I have a dream to change the starving little people.
Poor people, poor people.

Food is like their target to get,
The poor people are suffering,
We are living like kings to them.
Poor people, poor people.

Stop poverty! Stop hunger!
Some of them are living on the streets.
Stop poverty! Stop hunger!
They are all begging at our feet.

Give them food, give them water,
Don't put them towards slaughter.
Poor people, poor people.

Anna Povey (12)
North Walsham High School, North Walsham

Iraqi Government

This is why we are fighting,
These people are killing their own.
Others try to help
But they refuse them -
It's a scary haunted house
That frightens you to death,
It's as dangerous as a shark.
They're scared to go outside,
In case they are shot.
They need someone who is concerned,
They need someone who cares.
Their government needs to be re-formed.
They should be able,
To speak out for what's right.
The Iraqi people should be free!

Kellie Ackerman (12)
North Walsham High School, North Walsham

How To Change The World

H ave a dream
O f good things
W henever you want

T hink
O pen your eyes

C hange is good
H elp others
A lways
N ever give up
G ive it your all
E quality is needed

T ry your best
H ave a goal
E scape the world

W hich holds you back
O pen the door
R eward people all around
L ive life to the full
D reams are never too big.

Jake Isbell (13)
North Walsham High School, North Walsham

Racism

Racism rips relentlessly through nations and communities
Racism is a monster consuming our society
Racism is like a disease spreading, crippling, killing
Racism slashes through friendships like a knife
Racism starts wars as communities fight to be the best

Ferocity and fury lead to fear
Arrogance and animosity lead to attack
Torture and terror lead to trauma.

Thomas Belshaw (12)
North Walsham High School, North Walsham

Global Warming

It is life-changing.
Do you know about it?
It is like a greenhouse!
Global warming is destructive.

The atmosphere is burning.
Do you know about it?
It's breaking all the time!
Global warming is destructive.

It is vicious.
Do you know about it?
It will kill you!
Global warming is destructive.

You are causing this.
Did you know that?
Will you recycle?
One action could save so many lives.

Naomi Myhill (12)
North Walsham High School, North Walsham

Litter

I wish one wish, that litter was gone
Because it is so very wrong.

There is a thing, that's called a bin,
That is there to put things in!

Litter lies on the ground,
Slowly turning into a mound.

Litter is a huge mess,
If only there was so much less.

Less and less I wish to see,
Better then the world would be.

Rhiannon Dack (11)
North Walsham High School, North Walsham

Power

They have the one thing
That changes our lives
And the way that they use it,
Is worse than their hundreds of lies.

Their half-witted decisions
Destroy many nations
Beyond salvation,
It's disgraceful.
They make you feel like a lower
Power.

They have the one thing
That changes our lives
And the way that they use it,
Is worse than their hundreds of lies.

Their efficiency is incompetent,
They jettison others' ideas.
They've been at it for years.
So stand with me, at this glorious hour,
Power.

They have the one thing
That changes our lives
And the way that they use it,
Is worse than their hundreds of lies.

Power.

Power!

Luke Mulloy (13)
North Walsham High School, North Walsham

Being Treated Fairly

There are many people in our world,
Many are treated very differently.
Black and white,
Fat or thin,
Poor or rich.
The world is like a stormy sea, you may sink or swim.
I would like to change the world, to make it a better place.
I would make men to cook,
And women to play sports.
Black and white people would have the same privileges.
To be fat is not a disease but a problem that can be changed.
Being too thin is not healthy.
Being rich gives you more opportunities,
But having to be poor doesn't have to change or ruin your life.
Being treated unreasonably is infuriating.
Everyone should be treated the same,
No matter what you look like or feel.
If people could look through all that
They would see a wonderful, kind person
With many great qualities.

Thomas Baldock-Yaxley (12)
North Walsham High School, North Walsham

I Have A Dream

I have a dream
That all bad things will stop
Some things have
But poverty has not
It is as deadly as disease
Innocent people are starting to suffer
They are dying of thirst and hunger
Some have died, some are dying now
And for people in the world
This needs to stop now!
Why? Why, are they victims of this?
The world needs to stop all this
If we all work together
Things in the world will get much better
Giving money will pay for things
Food, water, it will bring
So that is my dream
For poverty to end
Please give money,
You will help a friend!

Chloe Bridges (12)
North Walsham High School, North Walsham

I Have A Dream!

I have a dream
That all animal cruelty is gone.
The everyone worked as a team
And the animals were set free.

The bear dancing as cruel as it is
And the horrible sound of the rattling chain.
That makes my nerves shoot up on end.
Why can't the torture stop?

The hunting and the death
Of the beautiful endangered animals
From tigers to pandas
Used for different things

Endangered to dangerous
Kept in cramped horrible conditions
For the rest of their lives.
When does the torture stop?

But on the bright side of things
For the animals' sake,
The RSPCA and the WWF and others
Are there to stop it now.

I have a dream
That all animal cruelty is gone.
The everyone worked as a team
And the animals were set free.

Jack Cresswell (12)
North Walsham High School, North Walsham

Stop Drink Driving

Stop drink driving
People could die
Stop drink driving
It's a deadly crime!

S top drink driving
T eenagers beware
O ne more won't hurt
P erhaps it won't be fair.

D on't end up regretting
R isking others' lives
I n the club you go
N ow don't get involved with knives
K ids get hurt, families start crying.

D rinking all night long
R efreshments won't do
I t's time to go at last
V ulgar behaviour starts, you too
I n the car you get, to the streets you go.
N ow are you . . .
G uilty or innocent?

Stop drink driving
People could die
Stop drink driving
It's a deadly crime!

Francesca Lee (12)
North Walsham High School, North Walsham

This Can All Be Changed

Smacking, slapping and screaming at children,
This can all be changed,
Children get beaten and belted and get black eyes,
Children want love and friendship, not danger and hurt.

Children get bruised and attacked,
Parents say they fell,
A little girl was playing with her toys,
So her parents decided to spank her hard,
She started to wail, so her parents hit her more,
The little girl turned black and blue,
Eventually her parents stopped,
And then locked her in her room,
But this can all be changed.

The wind was howling loud last night,
One mum couldn't take it,
So she clawed her daughter all night long,
Until the wind had stopped,
Smacking, slapping and screaming at children,
This can all be changed.

Rebecca Pratt (12)
North Walsham High School, North Walsham

I Had A Dream

I had a dream
That there was world peace
That there was no longer starvation
Or people suffering
Why is there war?
It's wicked and wrong, and no one benefits.

I had a dream
That there was no murder
Like someone had stopped it all, but how?
Global warming was no more
No evil death coming to swallow up
All living creatures.

I had a dream
People did not drink
No fights in the streets
No threatening drug ruling people's lives.

The world was fine in my dream.
        Why won't it happen?

Beth Bridges (12)
North Walsham High School, North Walsham

I Have A Vision

I have a vision
to win a crusade against animal cruelty
to stop animals' agony.
How would you feel
to be starved or beaten
with many bruises and to never have eaten?
It's barbaric. It's irrational.

People only do this
because they're pathetic.
disordered, demented or mad
or simply inhumane.

Last year
someone tied a hamster
a helpless hamster
tied it to a firework.
That gormless fool was arrested.
It was barbaric. It was irrational.

If you were a helpless animal
wanting a home,
but was treated like dirt
by some evil person.

Join us to end the pain
and to help the helpless animals
get the care they deserve.

Ben Chopping (12)
North Walsham High School, North Walsham

I Have A Dream

I have a dream
for tomorrow
that everyone will live as one
in a land
away from worries
where no wrong is maliciously done

Pink fluffy bunnies
roam the land
jumping through the green, green grass
everyone cares
they care for the world
and don't let off any greenhouse gases

No one is rich
no one is poor
everyone lives together in peace
no one controls
no one serves
and eternal joy will never cease

I have a dream
for tomorrow
about Heaven, it's not as hard as it may seem,
it is a land
away from worry
but right now, it's just a dream!

Lisa McIntyre (14)
Perth Academy, Perth

I Have A Dream . . .

I have a dream that,
we will live in a world,
without fear,
without violence, without bullies,
without discrimination.

I have a dream that,
everyone has equal rights,
that no one is killed because of their beliefs,
or the colour of their skin.
That,
one day,
everyone will join hands and say,
'We are proud to be human beings.'

I have a dream that,
no children will have to wake up to the sounds
of bombs and screams of people,
and to see the fear in their parents' eyes,
wondering if their family will be next.

I have a dream that,
everyone will be peaceful and friendly,
that there will be no hatred,
in our world,
that we all share,
equally.

I have a dream that,
everyone remembers the world is here,
for us all.
My dream may be farfetched.
It won't happen,
in my lifetime,
but . . .

I have a dream that,
one day my dream will come true.

Eilidh Marnoch (13)
Perth Academy, Perth

The Dream Divide

Peace on Earth
A large chocolate ice lolly
People smiling
A new PlayStation game

Happiness for all
Designer trainers
Harmony
Lots of money

Enough water to drink
The latest football strip
Something to eat
A brand new skateboard

A chance to learn
A Sony Erikkson mobile phone
A book to read
A plasma screen TV

Equality of opportunities
A new iPod
Hope
To stay up late
To sleep . . . in peace

Where in the world are you?
Why does it have to be so?
If just doesn't make sense . . .

Why have we built a world with such a divide?
Let's take it apart bit by bit
We can make it whole again
Believe and dare to dream
We can make it happen.

Holly Hunter (14)
Perth Academy, Perth

I Have A Dream

('Revive')

I have a dream . . .
That one day the sky will be pure
The jigsaw puzzle clouds
That piece together the sky
Will soon be
White.

I have a dream . . .
The sun
We can only hope that it has not,
In 20 years time, melted
Everything,
But still burns brightly in our sky.

I have a dream . . .
That the red chestnut tree,
That stands alone,
Proud and unique,
Blowing in the wind,
Does not get slaughtered.

I have a dream . . .
That the blanket that covers the night sky,
The sheet of black, which
Shelters the world,
From the universe around it
Remains.

I have a dream . . .
There is no death, but . . .
With no death, there is no sadness,
With no sadness, there is no world, and . . .
With no world there are no dreams!

Whatever you dream,
It is not wrong or right,
The dream is true when you believe in it.

Never stop dreaming.

Lisa Scrimgeour (13)
Perth Academy, Perth

I Have A Dream . . .

I have a dream that some day . . .

The world will be free from poverty.
Children in Africa will not go to bed starving,
they will have fresh running water.

I have a dream,
that the people of Africa will not suffer
from AIDS or any other diseases.

I have a dream,
that we will be able to hear children
laughing and playing with their families,
but instead we hear children
shedding tears for their dying mothers.

I have a dream,
that the children will no longer have to raid
and search the streets for food.
That the children will no longer have to wear
shabby clothes that they happen to come
across on the streets.

I have a dream that some day
these children will be able to play games
in the streets. And even though these
children may be happy we can still
make a difference.

I have a dream,
that they will no longer have to suffer
the pain that society has caused.

I have a dream,
that together we can put this suffering
to a stop.

This is my dream.

Hannagh Dellanzo (13)
Perth Academy, Perth

I Have A Dream

I have a dream
That the world's a fair place
Everyone has food and money which they need.
That is my dream.

Stop natural disasters
And famine and drought
Instead, three meals a day
And clean drinking water

Education for children
A, B, C, D
Numbers past ten
Young geniuses unfound

Jobs for the needy
Money for the poor
Shelters for the homeless
And churches for God

I have a dream
That the world's a fair place
Everyone is catered for
That is my dream.

Christopher Martin (14)
Perth Academy, Perth

I Have A Dream

I dream that everyone
could be treated the same
instead of all this violence and pain.

I wish that poor people in countries
could eat and drink their fill
instead of being pushed around
and held against their will.

I hope that one day everyone
can put there differences aside
instead of them being far and wide.

I dream that children shouldn't
have to wander the street
for warm clothes, shelter,
and a bite to eat.

But, most of all . . .

I hope that in the end,
people like me writing about
all the wrongs in the world
will eventually stop!

Claire Dryland (13)
Perth Academy, Perth

I Have A Dream

I have a dream,
That the world will not be so unfair
Everyone will be as lucky as us,
God help them

Give them three meals a day,
As much water as they want,
Give them vital vitamins,
And clothes to keep them warm,

Education and jobs are a must,
But they have all gone bust,
I hope the wars will stop,
So homes will stay up.

I have a dream,
That we will help them
Give as much as we can
And we can make a difference.

Derek Chan (13)
Perth Academy, Perth

I Have A Dream

I have a dream
that everyone will have peace
that there will be no trouble
so we won't need police

I have a dream
that everyone will have food
so that they will be happy
and be in a good mood

I have a dream
that everyone will have a home
that will make me happy
as I'm writing this poem.

I have a dream.

Paul McPhee (14)
Perth Academy, Perth

I Have A Dream

I have a dream
for all people
that every seam
will heal

That every crime
and every sin
will be like mine
in the bin

That every death
will be without regret
and every birth
will flourish

That the world
will mould
into a big, fluffy
ball of love.

Joe Norris (13)
Perth Academy, Perth

I Have A Dream

I have a dream
That we will all be free
To do what is right
For others and ourselves

To keep the air clean
And to respect the environment
Save the endangered
Reduce pollution and revolution
Before the children
Never see a wild animal!

Lisa Bonthrone (13)
Perth Academy, Perth

I Have A Dream

(1st June 2006)

I have a dream,
That soon it will be over for her,
Her broken world will return to normal,
And she'll smile once again.

I have a dream,
That her troubles will be solved,
She will suffer no more pain,
And she will see a brighter day.

I have a dream,
That those around her will not abuse her trust,
And she'll keep strong throughout tough times,
And people will not judge her.

I have a dream,
That her wishes will become reality,
That nothing will disrupt her plans,
And her life will be filled with happiness.

I have a dream for *Kirsty.*

Kimberley White (13)
Perth Academy, Perth

Let There Be Peace

I have a dream
That one day
The air we breathe
Will be clean
There will be no more wars
But more forgiveness
In the world that we live in
The seas will be fresher
The sun will live on
The skies will be blue
And the grass will grow tall
The way that we live
Isn't so like this
So let's help each other
And start writing our list
Then do something that will help the world
So are you with me
In my team?
Yes, this is my dream.

Zara Khan (14)
Perth Academy, Perth

I Have A Dream

I have a dream where no one is poor
The rich give and the sad are happy.

But, families are dying and children are starving
And yet we sit at home and do nothing.
We should care, and our world should be happy
I have a dream.

Governments and war, nothing is helping
Money is needed and children are yelping.

Give some money, clothes or food
You can afford it, but people who can't, they still would.
Look around and count your blessings,
But ask for love cos that's what's missing.

We're sad when we don't get something
But when we get it, we want something else.
But yet people around the world
Are happy finding water in wells.

Find the love in your heart
And make dreams come true.
Special is the one who helps
And that someone could be you.

A dream to have fresh water, food and a home
Having their parents at night, instead of being alone.
Love is the ingredient to make this dream come true
I have a dream . . . do you?

Klycia Carvalho (14)
Perth Academy, Perth

I Have A Dream . . .

I have a dream
of a peaceful world
a world without violence
wars and killings.

I have a dream
of a world free from poverty
and this may seem
not short of novelty.

I have a dream
of a world with no starvation
a world like this
would be a celebration.

I have a dream
of a world without segregation,
religions keeping and holding
relations.

I have a dream
of a world in peaceful harmony
where the birds are singing
oh so charmingly.

I have a dream . . .

Fergus Gill (14)
Perth Academy, Perth

I Have A Dream . . .

I have a dream
that war, fighting and violence
and all fear and suffering
will turn into silence

I have a dream
that guns, knives and terror
and malice and viciousness
will be an error

I have a dream
that threat, death and crime
and anger and selfishness
with criminals doing time

I have a dream
that we can all live to love
and let the bad feeling wash away
let us listen to the force above.

Andrew Christie (13)
Perth Academy, Perth

I Have A Dream

I have a dream
Of being the boss
Leading the team
Running the show

I'll pull at the reins
Of what I am given
Leave nothing but stains
Of success where they lay

I will take the lead
While others follow
Give them what they need
For nothing in return.

I will be a household name
You'll see my face every day
I will play the game
And come out on top.

Mark Jackson (14)
Perth Academy, Perth

Stop!

Following dreams,
Is up to oneself,
With no action,
Will wield no results.

If you follow your heart,
Be prepared
For the changes
That may come.

It may be your dream,
To win money, beauty or
Valued possessions,
But think what else you can do.

Stop crime and abuse
And help others

Just think what your dream could be!

Louise Littlefair (14)
Perth Academy, Perth

I Have A Dream

I have a dream
Of a peaceful
Free place

Where my worries
Are lost
And I feel at home

Things go back
To how they used to be.
Just turn back the clock.

I want to forget it all
Happened.
Leave it in the past.

Look forward
To a brighter day
When I can smile again.

Kirsty MacDuff (14)
Perth Academy, Perth

I Have A Dream

I have a dream,
What do you think?
Let's work together,
You could help me.

I have a dream,
What do they think?
If we work together,
We could be free.

I have a dream,
We're all part of it,
Listen to others,
Each one is unique.

I have a dream,
What would people think?
Maybe in some years,
Discrimination won't exist.

This sounds hard,
But here is the easiest part,
Share a smile,
Some day you could need one.

We all have this dream,
Is not easy to comply,
But as far as I know,
The main thing is to believe.

Maria Ignacia Troncaso Hugot (15)
Redland School, Santiago

A Perfect World

I suppose everyone wishes for a perfect world,
A world where everyone can walk the streets without fear.
A world where parents won't ever worry for their children when
they go out to play.
A world where no one dreads their first day of school or a new lesson.
Some people never smile in case it will be wiped away.
Some people stay sheltered in their homes in case someone hurts
them even more.
If I could change the world, no one would have heard of terrorists
and war.
Everyone would love each other and no one would be harmed when
they had their say.
No one would be labelled because of their religion or skin colour,
but because of their personality.
I hope the world will become peaceful and happy,
But only our actions will effect this.

Catriona Elliott (11)
Roundhay School Technology College, Leeds

I Have A Dream

I have a dream
that there were no wars
that fumes didn't poison the Earth
But I walk out of my door
I see all the corruption in the world.

I want to change that
I want to stop all crime
I have a dream
My dream is to stop the world from being corrupted.

Oliver Gularslan (12)
Roundhay School Technology College, Leeds

Dreaming . . .

Dreaming . . .
I dream that there will be no poverty in future generations.

Dreaming . . .
I dream that one day there will be no bullying or racism.

Dreaming . . .
I dream that terrorism will come to an end.

Dreaming . . .
I dream that war becomes peace.

Dreaming . . .
I dream that all countries join to become the world again.

Dreaming . . .
I dream that animals and humans are treated the same.

Dreaming . . .
I dream that dreams come true.

Emma Gilbank (12)
Roundhay School Technology College, Leeds

I Have A Dream

I have a dream . .
A dream to stop all racism!

I have a dream . . .
A dream to stop all poverty in the world!

I have a dream . . .
A dream to stop all wars!

I have a dream . . .
A dream to stop all fighting!

I have a dream . . .
A dream that everyone would get along!

I have a dream . . .
A dream that poor people were all wealthy!

Emma Harris (12)
Roundhay School Technology College, Leeds

I Had A Dream

I had a dream
That the future
Would bring happiness
And life

I dreamt that
There was no violence
No racism or cruelty
In the world.

I wish, I wish
No one was prejudiced
And everybody got along
That is what I would like
For the future we live in.

I hope that
For my children, and their children
The future will be bright
And that they will always be happy.

Kate Fraser (12)
Roundhay School Technology College, Leeds

I Have A Dream

I have a dream
That bad will be unseen,
Racism can have a permanent stop
With all that bad hip hop,
That prejudice can be wiped clean
So that it is nicely unmean,
I hope that war can be stopped
So we can jump and hop,
Wherever,
Forever,
Together.

Joshua Jones (12)
Roundhay School Technology College, Leeds

I Have A Dream

I have a dream,
The world is just about perfect,
No fighting, no killing,
But perfect.

I walk out my door and look into the sky,
No clouds appear and the sky is blue,
I hear the sound of birds singing,
Can't the world always be like this?
Don't you think this too?

I wish there was no war,
Wouldn't life be so pleasant without it?
Why do people do it anyway
And when will it stop or will it?

Will the world ever stop racism?
I wish there was a way for it to happen,
Just thinking about it, gets me angry,
I wish we could have a world without racism.

Haris Zubair (11)
Roundhay School Technology College, Leeds

I Have A Dream

I have a dream that one day we will live as one,
that there will be no such thing as bullying,
that there will be no such thing as terrorism,
that poverty and world hunger will be a thing of the past.

I have a dream that there will be no rich, no poor or popularity status,
we will all be equal, no matter what colour or religion we are.

I have a dream that all this can happen.

Charan-Deep Rathore (12)
Roundhay School Technology College, Leeds

I Have A Dream

I have a dream that
Soon, in the nearby future
Racism will be gone
There will be peace in the world.

I have a dream that
Racism will be forgotten
Everyone will treat each other for who they are
Like ordinary people

I have a dream that
All those killed by racism
Will be remembered for what they lived for,
Not what they died for.

Sophie Fielding (12)
Roundhay School Technology College, Leeds

I Have A Dream!

I have a dream.
A dream where there is no racism,
A dream where you are loved for who you are,
Not hated for who you are not.
I have a dream.
A dream where there is no war, only peace.
A dream where everyone is happy in the lives they lead.
I have a dream.
A dream for a great future for our children and grandchildren.
A dream where we live as one, not pushing people aside
                              from the group.

        I have a dream,
                  Don't you?

Emily Batty (12)
Roundhay School Technology College, Leeds

I Have A Dream

I have a dream,
A dream of a better world,
A world with no bullies,
A world with no unhappy child,
A future so cheerful,
A new dawn,
A new day,
A brighter future for the world.

No one should be looked down on,
No one seen as rubbish,
We shall not be judged by the colour of our hair or our skin,
The world will be a better place,
If you think of your fellow man
And lend him a helping hand,
Then put a little love in your heart,
And the world will be a better place,
For you and me,
Just wait and see.

Hannah Nota (12)
Roundhay School Technology College, Leeds

I Had A Dream

I had a dream,
About everyone being the same.
No one being judged
No matter what colour they are
No more racism
People getting along
Every person having the same rights.

Lewis Rudd (12)
Roundhay School Technology College, Leeds

I Have A Dream

I have a dream for aspiration of others,
inspiration to others and people to look up to others.

A dream where rare opportunities come up,
such as unity between all races of colour,
no teasing, bullying is gone and violence is forgotten.

A dream where there is no poor,
no rich, just fairness given with equality
through and through.

A dream of one light to share,
water to share, food to share,
poverty gone away.

A dream of only good influence,
change in life, and peace
finally ruling the world.

A dream where actions speak
louder than words and end
this political affair.

Priya Chohan (12)
Roundhay School Technology College, Leeds

I Have A Dream

I have a dream,
that there is no Third World,
that people do not go to bed starving for food,
the world is not full of evil, violence, racism and prejudice,
that the future will be hopeful for success and for me,
that there is no corruption in the world which we live in today.
I have a dream that we all come together and fight in the war
against evil and make a difference for the better.

Nathanael Clarke (12)
Roundhay School Technology College, Leeds

I Have A Dream

I have a dream that is so strong,
A dream that is out of control,
A dream that will change the whole wide world,
A dream that will regain lost souls.

Lost souls have been gone a long time,
Nothing beneath the skin and hair,
The person still walks, lives and talks,
But the personality is no longer there.

The reason for this is bad treatment,
Just because they are a different race,
Why does it matter to people so much,
That they have an original face?

Every single person is different,
Yet everyone should be treated the same,
They should be given the respect they rightly deserve,
Not because of their creed, colour or name.

I have a dream that is so strong,
A dream that will make things new,
I feel relieved because of one thing,
My dream is slowly coming true.

Megan Chitty (12)
Roundhay School Technology College, Leeds

I Have A Dream

I have a dream, like Martin Luther King
I have a dream, there is no war and guns
I have a dream, we can be all as one.

I have a dream, we live in peace and harmony
I have a dream, to grow and grow in what I want to be.

I have a dream, that the whole world reunites
I have a dream, that's why I wrote this poem at night.

Joshua Dunwell (12)
Roundhay School Technology College, Leeds

I Have A Dream

I dream of treats in restaurants
You dream of finding food in dustbins

I dream of party clothes
You dream of shoes without holes

I dream of being allowed to stay up late
You dream of a night's sleep without the sound of gunshots

I dream of family holidays
You dream of parents

I dream of going to school at Hogwarts
You dream of being able to read

I dream of a world where all children can dream children's dreams,
Not live my nightmares.

Lauren Gibson (11)
Roundhay School Technology College, Leeds

I Have A Dream

I have a dream that one day whom we admire,
Could truly inspire

Their example could fill us with ambition
And lead others to hold up their white flags in total submission,

As we look up with admiration
And possible change a whole nation.

From just someone we love and know
This is my desire,
To be inspired

From influence from a world leader or celebrity,
I also could motivate a whole city.

Leah Edwards (11)
Roundhay School Technology College, Leeds

I Have A Dream

I have a dream,
Where war is a thing of the past,
And peace is upon the world at last,

I have a dream,
Where poverty is no longer,
And we've said goodbye to aching hunger,

I have a dream,
Where the air is clear,
And polar bears can tread without any fear,

I have a dream,
Where no one is killed,
And the emptiness inside us has been filled,

I have a dream,
Where there is no sorrow
No war, no drugs, perhaps tomorrow?

I have a dream,
Where all this comes true,
And all it took was me and you!

Emily Esgate (12)
Roundhay School Technology College, Leeds

My Mum

She cares for me.
She feeds me.
She does everything for me.
She buys me anything.
She's rich.
She's pretty.
She's clean
And best of all, she is proud of *me!*
Just because she is *my mum!*

Nashila Hussain (12)
Roundhay School Technology College, Leeds

I Have A Dream

I have a dream of peace
A world where there's no enemy
A world where everything is nice.

I have a dream to make the world one
Where people do not consider differences
Between people's colour and culture.

I have a dream to let people be heard
To let people think whatever they want
To make their own decisions.

I have a dream where wealth is not considered
Where it does not matter how rich or poor you are

This is my dream, what is yours?

Salia Hanif (12)
Roundhay School Technology College, Leeds

I Have A Dream

'Vision is the art of seeing the invisible' by Jonathon Swift

Give me motivation from this hopeless situation
To believe in my abilities, to give some dedication
To find my strengths and weaknesses
To destroy everything that's meaningless
To achieve the best I can
To succeed with my own plan

To have a dream and see a vision
It all depends on my own decisions
To focus on what is right and keep my future looking bright
To have faith in life and trust one's might
I will not ever give up this fight.

Emily Short (12)
Roundhay School Technology College, Leeds

I Have A Dream

I have a dream,
Of a place without pollution,
Where we can live in harmony
And peace without commotion.

Stop killing the creatures
They have lives too!
I mean how would you feel,
If that was you?
All we want are their skins.
Just leave them alone,
Skins aren't worth lives
And neither are their bones.

The trees are going
But how can this be?
I mean, they're always growing.
It's actually you and me.
You may not have noticed,
But paper is wood.
You need to recycle
I think all people should.

This can all change.
It is my dream,
That fish will swim
In clearer streams.
The plants will come back,
Stronger than ever!
The rainforest shall stay
Forever and ever!
We can make this happen
If we all stick together,
Working hard with effort
And helping one another.

Gases will lessen,
The sea will be blue.
The Earth will be clean,
All shiny and new.

Cindy Lee (11)
Roundhay School Technology College, Leeds

I Have A Dream!

I have a dream
that my children and grandchildren will
be born into a peaceful world.

I have a dream
that the world will be peaceful
and there will be no such thing as wars.

I have a dream
that every race will be nice to each other
and not make racist remarks to each other.

I have a dream
that nobody will fight and carry knives
around like toys.

I have a dream
that there is no such thing as guns.

I have a dream
that one day we will work together
and we will make this dream come true.

I have a dream
we all should work together and bring
this world into a happier, peaceful and
nicer place to live in.

Tyron Jermaine Webster (12)
Roundhay School Technology College, Leeds

I Have A Dream

I have a dream that the world will be a better place.
People will be judged by what there is on the inside, not the outside.
No one will think bad things about themselves or anyone else.

Sophie Ruse (11)
Roundhay School Technology College, Leeds

My Mum

My mum is nice
My mum is sweet
Don't annoy her more than twice.

She tells me jokes
She makes me laugh
But she does not smoke.

My mum never frowns
She is a great woman
She will bring you up when you are down.

My mum's my mum
She is great
She is special
She is perfect
My mum's my mum.

Shaquille Morton (12)
Roundhay School Technology College, Leeds

I Have A Dream

I have a dream,
I dream for no racism in the world,
I dream for love in the world,
I dream for happiness in the world,
I dream for peace in the world,
I dream for no war in the world,
I dream for hope in the world,
I dream for bravery in the world,
I dream for harmony in the world,
I dream to eradicate poverty in the world,
But most of all I dream my dream comes true in the near future!

Ram Kalsy (12)
Roundhay School Technology College, Leeds

I Have A Dream

We want racism to stop
We want it to end
All races should be friends
No bombs or guns
Can't people just get on?
We are not that different
From each other.
So drop the guns and bombs
Drop the words, drop everything
A six letter word can start a war.
We all deep down,
Want to open a fresh new door.

Elizabeth Johnson (12)
Roundhay School Technology College, Leeds

I Have A Dream

I have a dream,
A dream of the world in harmony.
Without any violence or conflict.
Without any crime or chaos.

Only peace will flood the world,
Calmness and tranquillity,
Never will there be war again.

People in the world will foster new friendships,
And meet new people in the world.
In the world,
In a friendlier place.

Justin Lau (12)
Roundhay School Technology College, Leeds

I Have A Dream

A dream is the most wonderful thing that can happen to you
God's creation it is true
You can dream any time of the day
Dreams cause happiness not dismay.

A dream can be a wish that you wanna be
Like a tap dancer, ballet or street dancing but that isn't really me
It may not come true when you're older
But you did fight like a soldier.

A dream can be one of peace
One you like to cease
Like poverty throughout the world
That's what we like to see.

Amber Robinson (11)
The Streetly School, Sutton Coldfield

I Have A Dream

I have a dream,
I have a dream that one day I will be loved,
I'm fed up being told I'm loved
And then being given back,
When people are bored with me.
I have a dream,
I have a dream that one day I won't feel like a pass the parcel,
And one day I will be the prize
That somebody loves and treasures.
I have a dream,
I have a dream that one day I will have
A family that loves me,
And finally decide that they will keep me
And someone that I can call my own!

Kayleigh Middleton (12)
The Streetly School, Sutton Coldfield

I Have A Dream

I have a dream
That I will be rich
And marry someone
Who comes off a pitch.

I have a dream
I will get married,
Arrive at the church
In a five-star carriage.

I have a dream
I will go to space,
See the universe,
That would be ace.

I have a dream
That I will dance
All over the world,
Especially France.

I have a dream,
Go shopping every day,
Find fancy things,
Go and pay, pay, pay.

I have a dream
To live abroad
With my husband,
Who doesn't do fraud.

I have a dream
That wishes will come true,
See absolutely everything
That I want to.

Hannah Deakin (13)
The Streetly School, Sutton Coldfield

I Have A Dream

I have a dream,
That everyone makes a connection,
A bond, a link, a friendship,
No hatred, no poverty and nothing unequivocal,
Just tranquillity and serenity.
I have a dream
That everyone held hands and united,
Let war and execration be history.

People commit suicide, kill, die and murder
Just for money! How sad is that?
There is no point in racism,
Poverty and homelessness,
Is there?

I have a dream,
That just placidity spread around the world,
That hatred was never discovered,
All we need to do is smile and be happy
So finally poverty *will* be history.

I have a dream, do you?

Jodie Edwards (12)
The Streetly School, Sutton Coldfield

I Have A Dream

I have a dream, to make poverty history
When it will end, it's the world's misery
I have a dream that everyone has money
Kids could have pets like a cute little bunny
I have a dream that is coming true
That one day soon children can come out of their homes
To look at the moon
I have a dream that one day children will go to their moms
And say, 'Mom, what is hunger?'

Hayley Peach (11)
The Streetly School, Sutton Coldfield

I Have A Dream

I have a dream . . .

That racism will go at a pace,
To disappear without a trace,
That religious beliefs
Will be a warm relief,
To everyone in the world.

Homeless people fill the country,
How sad it would be to be one,
We need to do something
To give them another chance,
To live their life through.

Poverty is a cruel thing,
With people living alone,
Dying of hunger,
Every minute of the day,
They need our help.

Ryan Davis (12)
The Streetly School, Sutton Coldfield

My Dream

My dream is that one day I will be well known
Maybe a famous person
But as I get older I will want to be something else
People think that you can't live the dream
Well if you try hard enough then you will reach it
So don't give up, keep on trying
And you will be happy for the rest of your life
Forget about the bills or anything in your mind
Just let it all go and you will live to be kind
So build up your hopes
And live your dream
And someday you will live to be Queen.

Beth Burgess (11)
The Streetly School, Sutton Coldfield

I Have A Dream

Some people's dreams are relaxing,
Some a little strange,
But mine is completely different,
I have a dream of a worldwide change.

A change to our daily lives,
In our actions and our words,
Also a change in where we live,
So we can at least hear the song of the birds.

Fumes are suffocating,
Cars are screeching loud,
The population's shrinking,
Of this world, are we proud?

World War I, World War II,
And I hope there'll be no three,
What is this world we live in?
Tell me honestly?

Sitting on a grassy hill
I had a chance to think a while,
I wish our world would make a change
That would really make me smile!

Samantha Holyman (11)
The Streetly School, Sutton Coldfield

Dolphin Dreamer

My dream is to swim with the dolphins day or night
It doesn't bother me
They might give one a fright.
I don't know where I'll swim with them
But I hope it will be somewhere nice.

Emily Freegard (11)
The Streetly School, Sutton Coldfield

I Have A Dream

I have a dream
To make this world better at night,
So people don't get a fright,
As they pass through their life.

The world would be a better place
Instead of pollution and disgrace,
Everyone would be happy
And nobody would be upset.

Many people have dreams
That they were in a good team,
But that's just a load of rubbish,
My dream is unusual.

I hope this dream comes true
I really, really do,
Oh please,
That is my dream.

Zoe Darby (12)
The Streetly School, Sutton Coldfield

I Have A Dream

I have a dream that . . .
The world would be filled with peace,
There would be no pollution and no crime,
Rare animals would no longer be rare,
There will be no poachers,
The sea would be filled with dolphins, fishes and whales,
Animals will live in peace,
Animals and humans will live together in harmony,
People will be kind, considerate and treat people equally.

Rachel Huckfield (12)
The Streetly School, Sutton Coldfield

I Have A Dream

I have a dream that you can't judge someone
By how they look, move or speak.
Please don't follow the crowd,
Be an individual, go to them,
Don't point or laugh,
Treat them how you'd like to be treated
Never judge a book by its cover.
People may point at you,
They're still the same as you,
They've only got a different colour skin
And how they walk and talk.
I have a dream that we should all be equal,
Don't have wars, don't have fights,
We are all equal, don't have guns or knives
Just because they believe in a different religion
It does not mean they're different.

Jack Salter (12)
The Streetly School, Sutton Coldfield

I Have A Dream

I have a dream,
A wonderful dream,
To make every living thing
As rich as can be.

No animal cruelty,
New human rights,
Woodland parks
For the beautiful birds.

Maybe my dream will come true,
Maybe it won't come true,
But still the world revolves
Around me and you!

Grace Clusker (11)
The Streetly School, Sutton Coldfield

Dolphin Lover

I have a dream
A song to sing
I would help everyone and everything
I would help people through the night
So that they wouldn't get a fright
I turned on the light
So I didn't have a fright
Then I had another dream
It was great but I didn't have a debate
It was about dolphins
I love them
I want to swim with them
I wish I could
I saw a little light
It was so bright
Just thinking of my dream makes me cry
But it doesn't bother me
It's my dream!

Rebecca Snow (11)
The Streetly School, Sutton Coldfield

I Have A Dream

My dream is to make the world a better place,
To get racism out and peace in.
It doesn't matter what colour skin you have,
Whether it is black, white, red or blue,
If you're Christian, Muslim, Jew or Hindu.
I want no people to be homeless,
It will be peaceful,
Listen to what I say,
Let me change the world today.

James Duff (12)
The Streetly School, Sutton Coldfield

I Have A Dream

I have a dream
That one day there will be no violence, guns and war
That all countries will have peace
And no one will break the law.

I have a dream
That no matter what skin colour you have
Everyone will be treated equally
Because we really are.

I have a dream
That in Africa no one will starve
They will have enough food and water
And there will be no death.

I have a dream
No one will be on the street
No more begging
Everyone has a bed to sleep in.

I have a dream
That special needs children
Will be helped as much as possible
And can learn like us.

If this world was real
Everyone would have a meal.

Ben Perry (11)
The Streetly School, Sutton Coldfield

I Have A Dream

I have a dream
An everyday dream
To do something good
For me and my family.

To make peace in the world
Where everyone is the same
No one is better than someone else
And no one makes fun of anyone else.

Where everyone uses the same transport
No cars to pollute the skies
No pollution to cause global warming
And no icebergs to de-ice and cause floods.

No woodland parks to be knocked down
And cause the birds, insects and little animals to have no home
Left roaming, trying to find a new home
Getting run over by cars, left flattened in the road.

This is my dream
I hope it happens
And there is peace in the world
Where everyone is the same.

Sophie Fisher (11)
The Streetly School, Sutton Coldfield

I Have A Dream

I have a dream that all the world is in peace.
Everyone is happy, no one is sad or hungry.

But then I wake up and I see war, liars and sickness
Which no one can cure,
But there are people who are trying to stop everything bad.

But I wish with all my heart that the dream will come true,
At the moment everyone is thinking about money
And bringing sadness to people's lives.
Sometimes I wish that someone would bring the answer.
To help us save the world.

But saying that things are happening to make it come true
With people doing stuff like Live 8 and Make Poverty History
But we do invade this world
And now we have invaded it too much
We can't do anything about it.

I have a dream.

Charlotte Craddock (12)
The Streetly School, Sutton Coldfield

I Have A Dream

I have a dream . . .
One day I wish every person will have somewhere to live.
More people will give.
There will be no more people on the street.
Someone will always lend a seat.

Homeless people will be no more.
No sleeping on the floor.
Every person in the world will have a home,
Maybe even a garden gnome.

So every person in the world hear what I say.
Listen to me and help me change the world today!

Scarlet Bowles (11)
The Streetly School, Sutton Coldfield

I Have A Dream

I have a dream,
That one day everyone will be the same,
Black or white.

I have a dream,
That one day two people can pass each other in the street,
Without thinking something bad of one another.

I have a dream,
That one day there will be no hatred in the world but peace,
No more wars, no more fights,
But parties and celebrations.

I just dream,
That one day all there is in the world,
Is love!

Emily Rees (12)
The Streetly School, Sutton Coldfield

I Have A Dream

I have a dream . . .
My dream is that Mum and Dad don't shout
And my friends don't squabble,
But life is not perfect.

I have a dream . . .
That everyone likes everyone
And the Earth is clean,
But life is not perfect.

I have a dream . . .
That old people are nice to young ones
And Earth is calm,
But life is not perfect.

Lucy Worrall (12)
The Streetly School, Sutton Coldfield

I Have A Dream

I have a dream
That everyone could be equal
And black and white won't have to fight.

I have a dream
That people wouldn't fear to walk down the street
And go to their local shop.

I have a dream
That people would feel safe in their own community
And wouldn't fear to go on a bus.

I have a dream
People wouldn't fear to speak out loud
And that they would feel free.

I have a dream
That one day I could see around me,
A mixture of black and white people
And they would get along with not a care in the world.

I have a dream
That people white and black would share the same bus, car,
Street, shop or building with them feeling free.

I have a dream
That black people would be allowed to talk to white people
And also maybe form a relationship.

I have a dream!

Cree Lake (12)
The Streetly School, Sutton Coldfield

I Have A Dream Of A Dream World

I have a dream that poverty is a thing of the past
People have money to live
Charity give and help with kindness
People generally give up their time
To help the people living in grime.

I have a dream that racism is a thing of the past
Black and white, bound together as friends
Black and white treated the same
And no different in the way they are
After all we are all global citizens
I have a dream that war is a thing of the past
No one will die, people will last,
People won't have to cry.

I have a dream that child abuse will be a thing of the past,
Kids attacked and battered,
To other people it wouldn't have mattered,
Kids stranded on the streets,
Begging people who they meet.

I have a dream that child labour is a thing of the past
Kids sweat before they eat,
Falling down at their feet,
Don't people know that this is wrong.

My dream could help the world,
So a happy story could unfold.

Charlotte Turner (12)
The Streetly School, Sutton Coldfield

I Have A Dream

I have a dream and that is at every school I have been to
I have friends who have special needs such as dyslexia
Who are the same age as me!
I want them to have what I have,
They do get special lessons to improve their sight,
They never surrender, they're prepared to fight.
I want them to have what I have,
They do get games lessons but still have help.
They only need help to read and write.
Not to have fun and play with us.
I want them to have what I have, and that's freedom!
Everyone should be treated the same,
Not differently and helped also by others who suffer the same.
So they still get helped but altogether
So each other can help one another.
It does not matter whether they're disabled, dyslexic or blind
Everyone can have fun, friends and be treated the same.
That is my dream, my special dream, it will not change!

Jack Fleming (11)
The Streetly School, Sutton Coldfield

I Have A Dream

I have a dream that racism will stop
whatever black or white we are all in the same country
and I don't know why some people say racist comments
when they can always say something back.

Everyone will read,
everyone will write,
this will not give you a fright
even though you are a little tight.

The world would be a special place
I want no people to be homeless.

Daniel Whitehouse (12)
The Streetly School, Sutton Coldfield

I Have A Dream

I have a dream that everyone is the same
It does not matter if their skin colour is different.
There is more than racism,
Like poverty, AIDS in Africa and special needs.

In China there is child labour
And women who cannot have too many babies.

It does not matter if we are poor or rich
Or a different religion or race,
We are all equal.

Food shelters for the homeless need to be better
But we need to use what we have got.

OAPs are not getting enough help off the government
All the support is slipping.

Many people are mean and do not look at all the bad things
They always think about themselves and not others.

Shaun Wark (12)
The Streetly School, Sutton Coldfield

I Have A Dream

I have a dream
and that dream is that the world will have one person
who will change the world forever.
This person will give food and water to Third World countries
and make poverty history,
make people feel better than they really are
and make other people realise that they're not better than anyone else.
This person would stop racism, homelessness and child labour.
This is the sort of person we need to have in our world,
one who will change the world.
This person has feelings. Think what you can do to the world
to make it a better place?

Sarah Arrowsmith (11)
The Streetly School, Sutton Coldfield

I Have A Dream

I have a dream that not a thing went wrong
And so that everyone could walk whilst singing a song
War is so spiteful, horrible and mean,
Why don't we wipe the slate and start from fresh, clean.
Black, white, what difference does it make?
Why can't we quarrel when something more important's at stake?
Think of the people that are not only homeless
But sorry to mention, clothless.
Think of the people that have lost loved ones
And who can't hold their head high and sing some songs
Now just think how fortunate we are
And does it really matter what religion some are?
But realistically we are all the same
And all we have is different qualities, so some claim
So when you fall out with your mom and dad,
Just think you're fortunate and the world
Is full of people who are so sad.

Matthew Nutt (11)
The Streetly School, Sutton Coldfield

I Have A Dream

I have a dream that all racist comments stop now,
I wish that all poor countries will get treated like the rich.
I dream that poor countries will get donated a load of money.
I dream that people in poor countries will get doctors
So the population stays up.
I dream that countries will not have wars.

I have a dream that people will be treated the same.
I have a dream that there is no bad.
I have a dream that all countries come together
And settle their differences.

I have a dream that all people with disabilities
Could get treated so they are not down.
I have a dream that all the homeless people will have houses.

Ryan Bramwell (12)
The Streetly School, Sutton Coldfield

I Have A Dream

I have a dream
That one day there will be world peace
And that everyone will join together to be one

I have a dream
That people wouldn't be as daft as a brush
And respect each other for who they are

I have a dream
That soon, the grass will go green
And the sky will clear

If this dream would come true
Earth would be a different place
Everyone would get along, no racism

This dream may not come true
But we can still decrease the amount of racism
Together!

Arjan Mangat (12)
The Streetly School, Sutton Coldfield

I Have A Dream

I have a dream that poverty will come to and end,
Even with all the stuff we send,
It's not enough and it's not pretend.

People take their lives for granted,
But it's not their fault
And it's not what they wanted.

Why do people have to die,
When some people don't even try?

So how can we help their poor souls,
Give them loads of money and lots of gold.

Rhys Guy (12)
The Streetly School, Sutton Coldfield

A Better Place To Be

I have a dream that one day everyone will be equal
Crops will grow and water will flow
Every face I meet would smile at me
No matter what colour, face or gender
No matter what we think we would care for each other.

Bullies would stop and make friends
Homeless would not be a word
Colour would not be a vision nor a thought
Everyone would look and feel the same
Countries would just have names
No bad comments would be made.

Everyone will read and write
Every face will have a smile
Each foot will have a distance to run
And we will all be able to go there.

Every child will have a childhood
Every pupil will have a school
Everyone will have a hug to go to
I want the world to be a better place.

Hannah Southall (12)
The Streetly School, Sutton Coldfield

My Dream

When I am older I want to be a footballer.
I want to live on Roman Road.
I want to have a lot of money and silver and gold.
I want to have a good-looking girl.
I want to play for the Villa.
I want lots of cars like a Bentley and a sports car.
I want to win the Premier League for Villa.
That's my dream,
I want, I want, I want!

Luke Ryan (12)
The Streetly School, Sutton Coldfield

Young Writers - I Have A Dream Future Voices

I Have A Dream

I have a dream
That different people grow happy together
And I have a dream
That there is no racism in the world

I have a dream
That people treat the world better
And I have a dream
That the world lives longer than humans

I have a dream
That there would be world peace
And I have a dream
That people come to their senses to stop terrorism

I have a dream
That there will be no homelessness
And I have a dream
That everyone is treated equally

I have a dream
What's your dream?

Kiran Gill (12)
The Streetly School, Sutton Coldfield

I Have A Dream

I have a dream to be a car salesman
Who sells cars and big white vans
And earns lots of money
That would be my milk and honey
This time next year I will be a millionaire
Cars like Ferrari F430 never get dirty
I will clean it until it shines
Because one day it will be mine
This time next year I will be a millionaire.

My millions of pounds!

Bradley Rice (13)
The Streetly School, Sutton Coldfield

I Have A Dream

I have a dream
That the grass will grow green
And the world will be clean,
That the trees will grow high
Up into the sky.
Why have people got to be racist, why?
Why isn't there peace between black and white,
Wouldn't that be a wonderful sight?
The world is a big fight.
I have a dream
That the world will be a nice place to be
And a very nice place to see.
Let us live together in peace and harmony.
I have a dream
That we can look into the sky,
And watch the clouds flow by.
Why can't the world have nice weather
So we can look around together?
I have a dream
That people can live as long as can be
And everyone can be free.
The world should be a happy place
And the world should live with each and every race.

Adam Jones (12)
The Streetly School, Sutton Coldfield

I Have A Dream

I have a dream
That one day in the future the world can pull together and work as one
People like Saddam Hussein and Osama bin Laden will see what's
Right and what's wrong in life.

I have a dream
That soon people will stop polluting the world that we live in,
By using their cars and they will start using their feet
Which will not cost them any money.

I have a dream
That one day the world will be fair and that men and women
Will get paid the same wages and the world will stop being sexist.

I have a dream
That some day soon the poorer countries like Africa
And South America will have proper houses to live in
And will get enough money to feed their families
And I hope that fair trade fortnight will be made into something
That will happen 24/7, 365 days a year, every year.

I have a dream
That people in foreign countries will stop cutting down trees
That are already animals' homes and will let them live their life
Without having to worry about becoming extinct.

Heidi McManus (12)
The Streetly School, Sutton Coldfield

I Have A Dream

I have a dream
That one day people will pay homage to the countryside
So the hills don't groan at the litter penetrating into the ground.
Will we still be green?

I have a dream
That people will live in peace, away from blasting bombs,
The fighting will cease; guns will become silent
No-man's-land will become everyone's land.
Let's give peace a try!

I have a dream
That there will be no poverty or begging,
Food will be shared and homes will be built,
All needs will be met from the wealth of the world.
Will the world be free?

I have a dream,
We can clean our world; extract the fumes and halt the heat,
Prevent the poisonous arrow from piercing the clouds,
Make the air our children's future.
Will we succeed?

Thomas Duggan (12)
The Streetly School, Sutton Coldfield

My Dream

England netball is my game
On the court, in the fame
All the lights flashing down on me
Running round like a bumblebee.

Playing matches every day
Winner is the word that we say
The ball flying through the sky
I got hit and got a black eye.

Wearing the kit that we love
Defenders jumping in the air like a dove
Catching, passing and some more
All we want to do is score.

Throwing the ball up the court
Everyone screaming, giving their support
The goal is scored, we've got possession
I love netball, it's my obsession.

England netball is my dream
Hopefully I will play for the team.

Alison Wright (12)
The Streetly School, Sutton Coldfield

I Have A Dream

I wish I could work in a salon,
Nails, hair, I love it all!
If height could show how much I love it,
The pile would be 20 foot tall!

I wish the world was full of love,
No war, fighting, no hatred,
Everyone smile please,
No sad faces!

I wish no one was racist,
The skin colour doesn't matter,
Everyone would accept black people,
And stop this racist chatter!

I wish girls would be treated fairly,
No sexism, no unfair play.
I just really wish it could all happen today!

I wish everyone could get on well,
Everyone just be friends,
No falling out
And if you do, everyone just make amends.

I wish, I wish, I wish that all my wishes would come true!

Emily Capener (12)
The Streetly School, Sutton Coldfield

I Have A Dream

'I have a dream ...' was a famous speech

Hundreds of people listened to Martin
A man that stood on a box in the USA
Very strong to
Every person.

And after that, there was a lot less
Death due to racism,
Most or every person in the country was happy,
At the point of less
Mad, racist deaths.

All black people
Felt safer in their own homes
And on the buses and in shopping malls,
And everywhere else that
Our community likes to go under the sun.

Some people say that it was not mad,
But other people think it was extraordinarily mad.
Each and every person was thankful
Because Martin had a very strong feeling
And had the guts to get up and speak.

Sarah Evans (12)
The Streetly School, Sutton Coldfield

My Dreams . . .

In my dreams . . .
I love to be a dancer,
The best and well known,
Or maybe a singer that people admire,
Singing for everyone in the world,
The world will listen to things that are good,
No fighting, no violence,
Only things that are excellent.
We will work together, helping each other,
If the world was in tranquillity,
Instead of always conflict,
Then maybe dreams like mine
May have just a tiny chance.
So that's my dream,
Not for just me,
But for my world
And the people in it.

Alex O'Connor (12)
The Streetly School, Sutton Coldfield

I Have A Dream

I have a dream.
I have a dream that one day the world will be perfect.
I have a dream that the grass will be greener; the sky will be more blue.
I have a dream that the world will have peace.
I have a dream that we can go to other worlds.
I have a dream that people will live forever.
I have a dream that the world will be oh so clean.
I have a dream that the world will smell like flowers in the morning.
I have a dream that we will be allies with aliens.
I have a dream that I will explore the universe.
I have a dream that no racism or vandalism will be on the Earth.
I have a dream.

Jack Walters (12)
The Streetly School, Sutton Coldfield

My Dream

I have a dream
That every race will be equal,
That no one should be racist or prejudiced.
It does not matter who you are or what you are,
But everyone is special, no matter what.
Everyone is equal in their own way.
There would not be anything between us,
No poverty, no discrimination, no hatred,
There should be world love and peace.
No one should be dismal, in the doldrums
Or even crestfallen.
Everyone should be fair.
That is my dream
And I believe it should come true.
I hope it does.

Meganne Cowley (12)
The Streetly School, Sutton Coldfield

I Have A Dream

I have a dream that all abuse to children and animals will stop,
People will be able to live the life that they want to live,
The homeless will be homed and found a job
So they can carry on being happy.
I have a dream that no rules/laws will be broken.
I have a dream that no one will be hungry and
No one innocent will be hurt, but criminals will be punished.
I have a dream that the world will be at peace
And people will be happy in life.
Children will stand up to their enemies and will not be bullied.
No one will be intimidated, they will do what they think is best
For them and their families.

Ella Shufflebotham (12)
The Streetly School, Sutton Coldfield

I Have A Dream

I have a dream,
That evil won't be seen
And the world will live in harmony.

When people fight they get hurt
Is that right?
When people die families cry
Is that right?

People are happy with peace,
So why is there war?
People hate war
So why does Bush like it so much?

If you want to stop war it won't work,
Because power hungry dictators rule the world!
And the only way to get your message across
Is by acts of drastic violence!

So I have a dream to stop war,
Without violence, without fights!
It will be hard,
But also be right!

Jake-Lee Smith (12)
The Streetly School, Sutton Coldfield

World Peace

I have a dream,
I wish the world would reunite as one.
The stars and the sun should shine,
And the world should be a radiant place to live.

Why do some countries fight?
Can't everyone just get along?
Everyone has a right
To believe what they want.

There would be world peace forever,
Why are there wars?
War shouldn't happen - never.
Do people enjoy them? I don't.

I wish the world was cheerful and peaceful.
We are all blessed with life.
Our lives shouldn't be dispirited and dull,
Our lives should be ecstatic, festive and full of joy.

Everything is different and special in its own way.
We are all an important part of the world.
If we are kind and believe in ourselves every day,
There may be *world peace*.

Megan Phillips (12)
The Streetly School, Sutton Coldfield

My Dream

All around the world people are sleeping,
Sleeping in warm, cosy beds at night,
No one shivering in the bitter cold,
No one with no food to eat.

Everyone contented, cheerful and joyful,
No starving young children
Wrapped in a stingy, thin little blanket,
Dressed in rags, no money, absolutely nothing,
Everyone clean, everyone neat and tidy,
No one with straggly, filthy hair.
Hair just like straw.

Everyone living in peace and tranquillity,
Not having to keep an eye out for thieves,
No one should be dolorous, despondent or heavy-hearted,
Everyone should be exultant and starry-eyed.

Starry-eyed like an angel living in Heaven,
Everyone with shelter and a humble home,
Not living in the dismal rain and wind,
Catching pneumonia in the freezing weather
Or lying naked on the ground.

On the ground in Africa, cramped up with lots of people,
Suddenly I feel myself rustling
Under the covers of my comfy bed,
I wake up, where am I?
I realise I'm in my bed.

Oh my God, it must have been a dream!
I wake up, I see that I'm back in reality,
My brain springs into action, oh no,
There are homeless people all over the world,

Why can't everyone have a house to live in?

Laura Patton (12)
The Streetly School, Sutton Coldfield

Future

In the future I would like
The world to be the peaceful type
So I can run around and play
And go to sleep at the end of the day

In the future there will be
No wars, no fighting for the eye to see
So I can sleep at the end of the day
Thinking peaceful thoughts all the way

In the future there will be
Lots of money for you and me
So I can spend all day and night
So I'll be happy for the rest of my life

In the future there will be
Hovercraft for us to see
We will be happy with gadgets and things
We will even have laser keyrings.

Luke Mayo (12)
The Streetly School, Sutton Coldfield

I Have A Dream

I have a dream . . .
To be rich and to live in a mansion,
To own my own limo
And have my own driver in uniform,
To have as many pets as possible
And to be the greatest hairdresser ever.

Vicky Thrasyvoulou (11)
The Streetly School, Sutton Coldfield

I Have A Dream

I have a dream for the world
That no one would think of
My dream is for friendship to last
For ever and ever

Friendship is very special to me
And the world
My dream is for countries
To not fight and become friends

The world is becoming a bad place
Since the bombs and wars have started
This all needs to stop right now
Can someone please talk to Tony Blair?

Why do the countries have to fight?
If we all said no to fighting
And yes to friendship
The world would be a brilliant place

I don't know why we have to fight
Because what is the point really?
All we're doing is offering to die
When we could be at home watching TV

My other point is to stop racism
What is the point of taking the mick
Out of different people?
There is really no point

Friendship is a proper present
For the world to take care of
If you have it and don't take care of it
You won't have it anymore

That is my dream
Do you have a dream?

Rachel Sheldon (12)
The Streetly School, Sutton Coldfield

I Have A Dream

The haze cleared,
The scene was showing its contents,
The alarms were screaming,
The distress call spreading,

And there is a man,
Dead, lying cold,
While the rest of us know
His story is left untold.

The truth is not yet known
How the man was shot,
The police crawling everywhere,
Trying to find the gun.

The story is told,
Out of nowhere they are stricken,
Knocked down by an unknown face,
Shot, dead, by a chicken.

We are not safe,
It is us that could be next,
Drugs, drink, they are the cause
Of the dreadful sin.

Now you see,
In this world there is no hope,
Drugs, racism and drink,
People dying for the dope.

The haze cleared,
The scene was showing its contents,
The alarms were screaming,
The distress call spreading.

I have a dream.
Do you have a dream?

Verity Peake (12)
The Streetly School, Sutton Coldfield

I Have A Dream!

I have a dream for the world
That no one else dare dream,
I dreamt the world was a better place,
That poverty was no more.

Water running from our taps
Going down the drain,
We waste the water from our taps
While others drink the rain.

Food is cooked that we don't eat,
Drinks are wasted too,
But while we sit and watch TV,
They sit and pray to you.

If we all took a step to help,
Children would not die,
Turn off the tap while brushing your teeth,
You know it could save a life.

The food you know you do not like,
Why cook it? It's a waste.
Save the food for someone else,
You know it all makes sense.

Shelter is our homes around us
That we take for granted,
We have brick walls, while they have tents,
We live in luxury compared to them.

Isabella Powell (12)
The Streetly School, Sutton Coldfield

I Have A Dream

I have a dream
That the world will be different,
No poverty, hardship or beggary,
Where the poor have clothes, food and water,
Houses, education and most importantly . . .
Happiness.
The most important thing in life is to be happy
Because if you're not happy, you're not living properly.
I have a dream
That the world will change,
Decrease in pollution and global warming,
Where wind power will rule above all others
And the world is not suffocating itself.
Less coal, oil and natural gas is used; if not, none.
This is my dream.

John Goodby (12)
The Streetly School, Sutton Coldfield

Unique

Spoke accurately,
True words,
Beautiful in language,
Symbolic leader,
Extraordinary idol,
Fought for justice,
An inspiration,
Martin Luther King

Shot

Lost without him.

Ethan Dean (12)
Tonypandy Comprehensive School, Tonypandy

Death Against Discrimination

'We shall overcome', these words he said
To shelter over the innocent dead,
To speak and tell about his life,
To end the racism, fear and strife.

He fought for other blacks' rights,
He would never give up his great fight,
He was a legend, a great person to blacks,
A lot of stress was shoved on his back.

'I have a dream . . .' almost fulfilled
Until the unfortunate day when he got killed,
He was shot down dead with a bullet in the head,
He will remembered forever as the greatest, enough said.

Blacks will remember him as the one who said no,
He will be remembered forever and more,
The whites, the blacks, can now be friends,
Now this racist world should soon come to an end.

Jack Thomas (13)
Tonypandy Comprehensive School, Tonypandy

A Great Man's Dream

He dreamed to seek the freedom promised to us;
Where people work together,
And love each other forever,
Where people like each other,
Whether they are black or white,
In a world where no one fights,
Where hatred is not a choice,
When will they hear the voice
Of the great man speak
About the dream he wants to seek?
His name is King,
Martin Luther King,
Who only wants to bring
Peace into the world.

Tamsin Jones & Hayley Boyce (12)
Tonypandy Comprehensive School, Tonypandy

I Have A Dream

Martin Luther King was proud,
The words he spoke were clear and loud,
Those words he claimed are still in the air,
Martin Luther King was willing to care.

This amazing man fought for black people's rights,
He tried and tried, day and night,
His dream was for racism to end,
He put the message clear to send.

He stepped out on this balcony to give his word,
He stepped out and got shot, you couldn't hear a bird,
That day was very, very sad,
All of his people were very mad.

Joel Davies (13)
Tonypandy Comprehensive School, Tonypandy

What If?

What if there was *no* racism?
How happy this place could be.
What if there was *no* violence?
We'd be happy and live peacefully.

What if the world was a bombing field?
All those bombs flying around,
We'd all be scared and petrified,
To even make a sound.

What if nobody made a stand?
What would have happened?
Would whites have taken the blacks' land?
Or maybe the entire world weakened.

What if Martin Luther King was still alive?
Without that gunshot he might have survived
A little longer so he said more
All about the things he did before.

Kara Griffiths (13)
Tonypandy Comprehensive School, Tonypandy

One Of A Kind

An eye for an eye leaves everyone blind,
Martin Luther King - one of a kind.
He stood alone,
On the throne,
Fighting for black rights.

An eye for an eye leaves everyone blind,
Martin Luther King - one of a kind.
He wouldn't give in
To any man whose skin
Was white or 'better than his'.

An eye for an eye leaves everyone blind,
Martin Luther King - one of a kind.
The protests weren't violent,
The blacks stayed silent,
Under King's control.

An eye for an eye leaves everyone blind,
Martin Luther King - one of a kind.
His admirable dream
That somehow would seem
To be unforgettable.

An eye for an eye leaves everyone blind,
Martin Luther King - one of a kind.
Free at last,
Free at last,
Thank the Lord I'm free at last.

Annwen Ellis & Alex James (13)
Tonypandy Comprehensive School, Tonypandy

A Single Fighter

A fighter,
A peaceful fighter
Who had a dream of peace and justice.

Walking, walking to find a world,
A world where people are equal,
No matter the colour,
No matter the race.

The dream of that world seemed closer when they spoke out,
Cried out about the treatment they had to suffer.

People, many people, black and white,
Gathered together to listen to his words of wisdom,
Hanging on every word they began to understand.

The struggle of this battle was not near to the end,
But justice was getting closer,
The blacks were allowed to vote.

This came at a price,
The life of a man who stood alone,
The man who said
No more.

Shot on the balcony while preaching wise words.
An eye for an eye leaves everyone blind.

Zoë Walters (13)
Tonypandy Comprehensive School, Tonypandy

Death Of A Legend

Martin Luther King was a legend,
He fought for what was right,
He followed his dreams,
Fought for them with all his might.

On 4th April 1968,
Doctor King awoke,
Taking a deep breath,
He was going to make a speech today,
The last one before his death.

He stepped onto the balcony,
The people cheered,
'He's the best,'
A man in the crowd raised a gun,
Shot him in the chest.

Rushed to hospital,
Struggled to be revived,
But an hour later doctors revealed
Doctor King had died.

The people were horrified by his death,
Both black and white,
Even though their hero was dead,
They still continued to fight.

Because Doctor King had shown them a dream,
A dream that could not be shattered,
The dream of equality,
They still had each other, that was all that mattered.

They still mourned for their hero,
Their hearts felt as though they were breaking,
For the death of a legend,
Martin Luther King.

Martin Luther King taught us that America
Is not about the blacks and whites,
America is about people with rights.

Rhiannon Evans (12)
Tonypandy Comprehensive School, Tonypandy

Martin Luther King

I have a dream
Where the words that were spoken
Of a legend that lived
Heart wide open,
Loved being black,
Fought for his people,
Stood up to the whites,
That's true and simple.

Wanted to change the world,
Shot, so cruel and absurd.

Stood on the balcony,
Blacks cheering,
You're the greatest,
You're the best,
There was a gunshot,
King was hit in the head.

Matthew Perkins (13)
Tonypandy Comprehensive School, Tonypandy

He Had A Dream

He had a dream,
Defeat racism,
Tyranny over the black nation,
He had a dream,
Took a stand,
Fellow man turning on each other,
He had a dream, peace for all races,
No separate places for separate faces.

Nicholas Hall & Lewis Davey (13)
Tonypandy Comprehensive School, Tonypandy

The Dream

I have a great and brilliant dream,
Where blacks and whites aren't torn at the seam,
Where love and caring will stamp out war,
And all the racism will be no more.
I am a man who will take a stand,
So that blacks and whites can walk hand in hand.
I am a man who would wipe the slate clean,
So that I can live my wonderful dream.
I'm proud to be black and who I am,
And I will help whoever I can.
I am a man who sees through the skin
And only sees the person within.
My words are true and they make you see
That whilst racism is about, there is nowhere to be,
Apart from scared and sat in your home,
Sitting there frightened all alone.
But together we can overcome,
And everybody can live as one!

Dale Stoddart & Sophie Harris (13)
Tonypandy Comprehensive School, Tonypandy

The One And Only

I have a dream to see this place
Growing in goodness, not in disgrace.
I have power over this land
To stop racism, to make a stand.

My words make people think
About how we could live in just one blink,
Not having to suffer, not having to cry,
Living a long life, not having to die.

There doesn't have to be fights,
Just plain human rights,
Black and white people are just the same,
But why do we all take the blame?

For the fighting lands on our shoulders,
But still it brings us down like boulders.
All the hope we should lend,
Let the suffering come to an end!

Sophie Evans & Jasmin Honeyfield (13)
Tonypandy Comprehensive School, Tonypandy

Immortal

An eye for an eye leaves everyone blind,
The wonder that transpires in a terrorist's mind,
Discrimination, assassination,
One big exasperation.

One man tried to defeat the racial hate,
Took an active part in every debate,
He was black and wouldn't accept
The pointless killing concept.

Spoke his mind, kept on trying,
To stop shots, knifing and bombing,
Persevered to change life,
In the course took trouble and strife.

His battle went on for years,
Though it all created tears,
People killed, houses kindled,
Children suffered, people crippled.

Stirred a nation's heart and mind,
Told that colour's not how we're defined,
His message is still clear,
His memory will always be near.

Could have hated, but he chose
To reject violence, to oppose,
Told to love and understand
The evil in our land.

Shot down dead on a balcony,
The way he died was uncanny,
Always spoke of his assassination,
Never resorted to retaliation.

Each year his birth's a holiday,
There's something I need to say,
The nation will always remember him,
We wonder when his dream at last comes true.

Leon Jones (13)
Tonypandy Comprehensive School, Tonypandy

Young Writers - I Have A Dream Future Voices

Forgiveness And Hope

I have a dream to see this place
Growing in goodness, not in disgrace.
I have power over this land
To stop racism, to make a stand.

Martin Luther King was a proud man,
He fought for right and had many fans.
Martin cared for his friends,
Many people drove him round the bend.

He wanted to make this world a better place
With happy with a smiley face.
The colour of his skin
Still made him win.

He sadly died with power and hope in his eyes,
In America, that's where he lies.
People will never forget him,
But he did forgive all sins.

Jordan Woodland & Sarah Tanner (13)
Tonypandy Comprehensive School, Tonypandy

I Have A Dream

I have a dream that one day you will not look at me
Through narrowed eyes or sideways glances.
Feeling your thoughts and taking your chances,
You may laugh, but you may cry,
Common rules that you abide by.

This long struggle is getting me down,
It's not a smile on my face, but yet a frown.
I wish I could run, I wish I could talk,
I wish for a mind of a knowledgeable thought.

As I scream you leave the room,
To wallow in my pity,
Drowning in my gloom.

My outlook on life is non-existent,
I wish the world would not be so resistant.

But I am still dreaming . . .

Dominic Lewis (16)
Ysgol Bro Gwaun, Fishguard

I Have A Dream

I have a dream
For a better world,
For future generations,
For a greater future.

I have a dream
For a cleaner world,
Without pollution,
Without complication.

I have a dream,
When will it happen?
We need it to work,
Work as a team.

Andrew Wells (16)
Ysgol Gyfun Llanhari, Pontyclun

I Have A Dream

My days are filled with dreaming
Of a warm and better place,
There all my worries are over,
And I have no problems to face.

My heart is filled with anger
And regret from time gone by.
Sometimes my fears overwhelm me,
And then all I can do is cry.

I can only dream of being happy
When I'm alone and wild and free,
But even then my fears will wait
To come back someday and haunt me.

My fears are horrible creatures,
Filled with self-pity, worries and dread.
They turn my world upside down,
And play havoc with my head.

Sometimes my dreams are overtaken,
By their enemy when I'm in my bed.
This can be the worst thing of all,
Because I can't forget what they said.

I hope one day they'll remember
All the bad things they did to me,
So that one day their hearts too, will be filled
With anger, regret and self-pity.

But for now I'll do my best to forget
Their tortures and evil torments.
I'll lock away all of the anger and pain
And forget my precious time that they spent.

Laura Rowlands (14)
Ysgol Gyfun Llanhari, Pontyclun

I Have A Dream

I have a dream that everyone is treated equally,
That people aren't bullied because they are different,
That people aren't teased for their style or interests.
I have a dream that people will just be themselves
And won't go along with the crowd,
That people aren't hurt or killed only because of the colour
Of their skin or their appearance,
That girls won't hate themselves because they aren't as skinny,
Pretty or popular as celebrities.
I have a dream that people will judge each other by their
Personality and character and not by what they see on the outside,
That everyone is allowed to be individual and different
And not become clones of the rest of the crowd,
That wars aren't caused by religion and all of us can have our
Own opinion on what religion, if any, we choose to believe in.
I have a dream that everyone will accept other people's religious
Beliefs and not protest against different religions because they are
Different to their own.
I have a dream that stereotyping, prejudice and discrimination
Are all non-existent so the world will become a better place.

Megan McCutcheon (14)
Ysgol Tre-gib, Llandeilo

Chilling

If only everyone could be happy,
This isn't always possible;
However there are things you can do,
To make someone feel special . . .

It's always good to feel calm and relaxed,
Through the hustle and bustle of life;
Escaping through the countryside may make someone
Feel like they're entering a totally different world . . .

Almost incredible but simple choices
In life can change someone . . .
A moment alone in tranquillity
Amongst the gentle waving branches of trees . . .

Gazing at the fluffy white clouds
Travelling across the skies,
The fresh smell of spring
Seeming inevitably comforting . . .

You can help,
Please recycle . . .
Don't be a culprit
And help someone feel different today!

Olivia Ng (14)
Ysgol Tre-gib, Llandeilo

My Dream That Everyone Is Special

I have a dream
That everyone is treated the same,
Whether they are short, tall, fat,
Thin, smart, able-bodied or even lame.

I have a dream
That no class systems exist,
That everyone is equal,
No one is on an invisible list.

I have a dream
That everyone is nice,
That differences are good,
No one is classed,
Including those who choose to wear a hood.

I have a dream
That no matter how important
People might think they are,
They will know that
Everyone is a shining star.

I have a dream
That most people might,
Everyone is happy
And the world is right.

Beth Pretty (14)
Ysgol Tre-gib, Llandeilo

The World

The world was a wonderful place,
When humans there wasn't a trace.

All over the world was peace,
Then we came and everything ceased.

We destroyed the forests and land
And killed off the dodos by hand.

We built roads, cities and cars
And tried to send rockets to Mars.

We're polluting the Earth's air
And most humans don't even care.

We're killing the animal race
And all of this death is a waste.

We've fished the sea of life,
Sea animals cannot survive.

When nuclear bombs were made,
We were digging the Earth's grave.

If we fire the weapons created,
The world will be cremated.

And no life will be spared,
Now I hope us humans are scared.

Jack Amblin (14)
Ysgol Tre-gib, Llandeilo

Mission Impossible

Black or white,
Jew, Muslim or Sikh;
We're all the same,
Not one of us a freak.

Bullies in the playground,
Threatening to fight,
Terrorising us all,
What gives them the right?

Freedom of speech,
Express what you may;
Is it really existent?
Or for this, will we pay?

Where is the truth
So deeply hid?
Lies from every direction,
Confusion, I'm stuck amid.

Forward as one,
The world united together,
But is there not still war and hatred?
Will peace be impossible forever?

This brutal and unfair world,
Power thirsty giants crushing and destroying,
While the Third World is left to rot,
Where's the compassion and brotherly feeling?

Respect is the key,
Prejudice must be abolished.
When all this is done,
My mission is truly accomplished.

Lisa Childs (13)
Ysgol Tre-gib, Llandeilo

I Have A Dream

If only there were harmony
Between the human race,
It wouldn't matter where you lived
Or colour of your face.

No wars, no guns, no chemicals,
Polluting people's minds,
But helping one another,
All faith, all race, all kinds.

The images of children
Who don't know when they'll eat,
We take it all for granted
As they scavenge on the street.

The poverty in Africa,
Do you think it's fair
That while they scrape a living,
Some don't even care?

All religions of the world,
In their own way tell a tale,
But conflict always will arise -
Why can't peace prevail?

Inequality across the world
Will always cause much pain,
But why does it still occur?
For we are all born the same.

I wish of a world that's full of peace,
Of people good, not bad.
And my hope is of love not war,
Then no one will be sad.

Jessica Fay Davies (14)
Ysgol Tre-gib, Llandeilo

All Alone

A boy walks alone in the playground,
He's got no one to turn to,
He stands alone,
No one wants to help him,
He's being bullied by older kids,
Others are too scared to get involved,
In case the bullies turn on them.

If someone could give him the courage
To stand up to the bullies,
To tell someone what's happening,
Then he wouldn't want to die,
He would lead a normal life,
Filled with happiness and glee,
Is that someone you?

A little girl cries into the night,
Because no one wants to be her friend,
She is black and they are white,
They can't see her from the inside,
Just take a minute to think about your actions,
And see the people that are hurt,
Maybe then the pain will end.

I have a dream that one day,
The people of the world will live as one,
That no one will feel miserable,
People will work together
To stamp out the sins of others,
And to work together as a team,
Instead of individually.

Catherine Spencer (14)
Ysgol Tre-gib, Llandeilo

I Have A Dream . . .

I have a dream that one day
People won't wear fur,
That celebrities don't wear it either
And animals aren't seen as clothes.

I don't see why Jennifer Lopez
Is so popular,
When most of the time
She's wearing animal fur!

She wears fur coats,
Hats, gloves and scarves,
Big boots too,
Out of gentle rabbits and foxes.

She owns her own 'fur farms',
Where animals are taken to be killed,
All the fur goes towards her coats,
How cruel can you get?

She sometimes wears false eyelashes,
Which I thought was quite cool,
Until I found out they were made from . . .
. . . real fox fur!

So, I figured out that
I don't like her any more,
I don't like cruel, evil and selfish people
And that's what she is: cruel, evil and selfish!

Nicola Gillings (13)
Ysgol Tre-gib, Llandeilo

If Only . . .

If only the sun shone every day
And nothing good would go away.
If only racism could fly away like a bird,
There wouldn't be another bad comment or word.
If only my children could live in a peaceful society
And no one would need to be hard or mighty.

If only all the animals could live
And all the people could get along and give.
But let's turn on the light now and wake up.
Maybe it's only in my dreams that this dream can come true
And make up a beautiful world like a potter may make a beautiful cup.

Bethany Elias (14)
Ysgol Tre-gib, Llandeilo

I Have A Dream

A dream is something you imagine,
Something that can work and even happen.

A dream is a utopian place,
There are no problems, none to face.

A dream is a paradise where everyone's free,
There is no black, no white to see.

A dream is a world that doesn't know poverty,
Where we don't have to come to terms with cruel reality.

A dream isn't a hellfire of cruelty,
War, corruption and full of catastrophe.

But, a dream will only stay as a dream,
If we, the world, don't work as a team.

Siôn Jones (15)
Ysgol Y Moelwyn, Blaenau Ffestiniog